D0820641

When Self-Consciousness Breaks

Philosophical Psychopathology: Disorders in Mind
Owen Flanagan and George Graham, editors

When Self-Consciousness Breaks

Alien Voices and Inserted Thoughts

G. Lynn Stephens
George Graham

A Bradford Book
The MIT Press
Cambridge, Massachusetts
London, England

© 2000 Massachusetts Institute of Technology

All rights reserved. No part of this book may be reproduced in any form by any electronic or mechanical means (including photocopying, record-ing, or information storage and retrieval) without permission in writing from the publisher.

Set in Bembo by Best-set Typesetter Ltd., Hong Kong.
Printed and bound in the United States of America.

Library of Congress Cataloging-in-Publication Data

Stephens, G. Lynn.
   When self-consciousness breaks : alien voices and inserted thoughts
   / G. Lynn Stephens, George Graham.
         p. cm. — (Philosophical psychopathology. Disorders in mind)
   "A Bradford book."
   Includes bibliographical references and index.
   ISBN 0-262-19437-6 (hc : alk.paper)
   1. Auditory hallucinations.   2. Thought insertion.   3. Self.
4. Self-perception.   I. Graham, George, 1945–   II. Series.
RC553.A84 S74 2000
154.4—dc21   00-026720

For nothing can be sole or whole
That has not been rent.
—W. B. Yeats

Contents

Series Foreword

The aim of this series is both interdisciplinary and uncharted: to offer philosophical examination of mental disorder, an area of intense and fascinating activity in recent years. The perspective of philosophy provides a richly synoptic vision of the forms, limits, and lessons of mental disorder, as well as of its study and its treatment. Potential topics include but are not limited to the following:

- how to explain mental disorder
- dissociative personality and volitional disorders and what they tell us about rational and moral agency
- the lessons of cognitive neuropsychology for the nature and function of mind
- whether disorders are "rational strategies" for coping with trauma or stress
- relations between dream states and psychosis
- neural-network models of pathology and their implications for the debate over the functional integration of mind/brain
- culture-specific and gender-linked forms of psychopathology and their lessons for the taxonomy of mental disorder and for the scientific status of the study of mental illness
- logical and epistemological relations between theories of mental disorder and forms of therapy
- conceptual and methodological foundations of psychopharmacology

• ethical and political issues in definition and treatment of mental disorder

We welcome proposals and submissions from philosophers, cognitive scientists, psychiatric researchers, physicians, social scientists, and others committed to a philosophical approach to psychopathology.

Owen Flanagan
George Graham

Acknowledgements

This book is thoroughly collaborative. The order of authorship was determined arbitrarily.

We received help from many people in writing this book. We wish to express our special gratitude to Owen Flanagan, Betty Stanton, and Amy Brand. We also wish to thank Carolyn Gray Anderson, William Bechtel, Paul Bethge, Stephen Braude, K. W. M. Fulford, Lisa Hall, Terence Horgan, Marcel Kinsbourne, and numerous other friends and associates who supplied forms of intellectual assistance. Specific intellectual debts to various philosophers and psychiatric professionals, when we can remember them, are acknowledged in the body of the text.

We extend our thanks to the Bellagio Residency Program of the Rockefeller Foundation, to the National Endowment for the Humanities, and to the faculty sabbatical leave program of the University of Alabama at Birmingham; to audiences at Duke, Georgia State, the University of North Carolina, Oklahoma State, Rutgers, the Universidad Nacional Autonoma de Mexico, Wake Forest, and Washington University; to members of the American Philosophical Association, the Association for the Advancement of Philosophy and Psychiatry, the Society for Philosophy and Psychology, and the Southern Society for Philosophy and Psychology; and to the Johns Hopkins University Press and the journals *Philosophy, Psychiatry, and Psychology* and *Philosophical Topics* for permission to adapt portions of the following articles:

"Voices and selves," in *Philosophical Perspectives on Psychiatric Diagnostic Classification*, ed. J. Sadler et al. (Johns Hopkins University Press, 1994)

"Self-consciousness, mental agency, and the clinical psychopathology of thought-insertion," *Philosophy, Psychiatry, and Psychology* 1 (1994): 1–10

"Psychopathology, freedom, and the experience of externality," *Philosophical Topics* 24 (1996): 159–182.

We are grateful to The MIT Press for allowing us to incorporate in this book material from "Mind and mine," published in the 1994 volume *Philosophical Psychopathology*, which we edited. (Although some sections of some chapters appear in different forms in the above-mentioned papers, the preponderance of the material in this book is new.)

Finally, but most important, we wish to thank our families for their love, support, and patience. To them this work is dedicated with affection and gratitude.

When Self-Consciousness Breaks

1

Introduction

1.1 Swallowing Candy

I'm 56 years old, stand 5 feet, 11 inches in my socks, weigh 165 pounds stripped, and am, so to speak, inside your head at the moment and speaking these words. I want you to get rid of the candy in your mouth. Did you hear that noise? That is the sound of candy—your candy—being swallowed. You have very good manners. Other people I know would have refused to follow instructions.

This book is about *that*. That is, it is about what happens when people think like the above: when they have the sense that someone else speaks or thinks within their minds.

What happens in such situations differs in an important way from the standard or normal experience of introspective awareness. "The universal conscious fact," wrote William James in the *Principles of Psychology* (1918, p. 226), "is not, 'Feelings exist,' or 'Thoughts exist,' but 'I think' and 'I feel.'"

According to James, introspection is standardly or normally a self-conscious experience. It involves more than noting the occurrence of particular thoughts or feelings. It involves being aware of thoughts and feelings *as* one's own: as things that I myself think or feel.[1]

Suppose that you are reading this book, attending to every word, and suddenly you shift attention from the object of your visual experience (the book) to *your* experience of reading. Suddenly, suppose, it seems to you that you dislike the book, that you had expected from the subtitle ("Alien Voices") to read a book on the role of alien space invaders in disturbances of consciousness. You feel disappointed, maybe even cheated. This is an example of being aware of your own feelings as your own. You are conscious of yourself as reading, as feeling disappointed, and as cheated. You are, in James's sense, self-conscious.

The experience of self-consciousness is universal (we all have it) but not communal (we never share it). No one can join you in your self-consciousness. You cannot join others in theirs. However, it certainly seems, when we turn to clinical psychiatric phenomena, as if things can and sometimes do become confused in introspective experience. To put matters provocatively: sometimes, when self-consciousness breaks down or becomes disturbed, it appears to the self-conscious person as if *other* selves or agents are involved in his or her stream of consciousness. Within introspective awareness, other persons seem to speak or think. Another's voice is heard: the voice of a 56-year-old in socks. Such provocation wants clarification.

A major part of developing a philosophical theory of self-consciousness is identifying the elements or dimensions of self-conscious experience. With some exceptions, the strategy

---

1. Occasionally, for stylistic purposes, we use the authorial first person pronoun.

employed by philosophers in developing the theory has been to examine self-consciousness under circumstances in which there is little or no stress or serious disturbance within a self-conscious person.[2] However, as William Bechtel and Robert Richardson note in *Discovering Complexity* (1993), unstressed or orderly psychological activities often conceal their component structures or elements. Overtaxed or disturbed activities, by contrast, may be more revealing of their constituents. "The breakdown of normal functioning," write Bechtel and Richardson (ibid., p. 18), "often provides better insight . . . than does normal functioning." So, examining self-conscious experience under conditions of stress or when it is disturbed may serve as an illuminating guide to components of self-conscious experience.

Studying the clinical literature on psychopathology raises questions about just what happens when self-conscious experience is disturbed. *Fish's Schizophrenia*, a clinical handbook, echoes James:

Thinking, like all conscious activities, is experienced as an activity which is being carried out by the subject. . . . There is a quality of "my-ness" connected with thought. (Fish 1962, p. 48)

However, Fish goes on to observe that, under certain conditions, this quality of my-ness vanishes, though introspective awareness of the thought itself remains:

In schizophrenia this sense of possession of one's own thoughts may be impaired and the subject may suffer from alienation of thought. . . . The patient is certain that alien thoughts have been inserted into his mind. (ibid., p. 48)

2. For representative examples, see Chisholm 1976, Chisholm 1981, and Shoemaker 1986.

In cases of this phenomenon (referred to in the literature as delusions of "thought alienation" or "thought insertion"), the subject reports that another's thoughts occur in his mind or stream of consciousness. To persons undergoing delusions of thought insertion, the experience of thinking is not "I think" but "Someone else is putting their thoughts in my head."

Nor is thought insertion the only, or the most common, case in which people experience their own thoughts as somehow alien. Sometimes subjects experience their own thinking or inner speech as "voices" or "verbal hallucinations." Here "I think" or "I say to myself" gives way to "I hear another speaking."

Thought insertion and verbal hallucinations are examples of what we wish to call *alienated self-consciousness*. By this expression we mean that they are experiences in which the subject is directly or introspectively aware of some episode in his or her mental life, but experiences the episode as alien—that is, as somehow attributable to another person rather than to the subject. No doubt there are other sorts of instances of alienated self-consciousness. Persons report alienated experiences of moods, emotions, and impulses. However, these two, and particularly verbal hallucinations, are by far the most widely studied and extensively described in the literature. For this reason, we shall make them the focus of discussion in this book.

1.2 What Is This Book About?

In this book we explore two sorts of questions about verbal hallucinations and thought insertion. The questions of the first sort concern what philosophers and others call *phenomenology* (in the broad and uncontroversial sense of this term). That is, they concern what experiences of alien thoughts in verbal hallucinations and thought insertion are like for their subjects. In what does their experienced alien character consist? How does the experience of an alien thought differ from the experience of a thought which a person regards as unproblematically his or her own? The questions of the second sort concern the implications of alienated experience of thoughts for our general understanding of self-consciousness. What features of self-consciousness make alienated experience possible? What, if anything, do verbal hallucinations and thought insertion reveal about self-consciousness, generally? Do they tell us anything about whether there are different dimensions or strands to self-consciousness, different otherwise normally unified elements in self-conscious experience?

We are philosophers. We don't see patients. Thus, in answering those questions we will draw freely and rely heavily on clinical and experimental literature in psychopathology, and not only for data (such as patients' self-reports and clinical descriptions) but also for theoretical analysis and insight. There are extensive overlaps, at least, between the two questions we ask and questions asked by mental health professionals. It is probably accurate to say that our concerns form a subset of the concerns raised in the literature on psychopathology about alienated self-consciousness.

Our concerns form a proper subset. The psychiatric literature addresses all the questions we raise, but we do not discuss all the many issues addressed in that literature. We say little about neurology and nothing about psychopharmacology. Although we discuss the general features of human self-consciousness that make possible alienated experience of one's thoughts in verbal hallucinations and thought insertion, we don't discuss the epidemiology or the social risk factors of the disorders. Nor do we advise doctors or patients about therapy or treatment.

More generally, our discussion differs in emphasis from most discussions of thought insertion and verbal hallucinations in the psychopathology literature. Those discussions typically deal with these phenomena in the context of mental disorder or disease. Does their presence serve as a reliable indicator of the presence of underlying pathological processes? What do they reveal about the nature of such processes? Do they provide useful guidance for differential diagnosis of, for example, schizophrenia or multiple personality disorder?[3]

It is not part of our project to criticize the medical approach to the study of thought insertion and verbal hallucination. We adopt a different but not competing or incompatible perspective. We are interested in what verbal hallucinations and thought insertion reveal about the underlying psychological structure or processes of human self-consciousness, not in what they reveal about the underlying pathology of mental illness. Whether the processes revealed are pathological, or whether they are characteristic of specific forms of psychopathology, is simply not close to our intellectual hearts in this book. In our discussion of the psychological processes that result in verbal hallucinations, we defend the view that verbal hallucinations do not occur exclusively in connection with mental illness. As we read the medical literature, this is a fairly uncontroversial position, and it is

3. There may also be differences in the vocabulary which we use to discuss thought insertion and verbal hallucinations and the language of some discussions of psychopathology. For example, where we speak of alienation, the psychopathology literature sometimes prefers to speak of "dissociation," although it is becoming increasingly clear in this literature that a concept like dissociation is too loose and semantically various to capture the unique features of alienated self-consciousness.

compatible with a variety of proposals regarding the significance of verbal hallucination for differential diagnosis.

1.3 Overview of Main Ideas

When William James—himself interested in philosophic implications of mental disturbance—contrasts my awareness that a thought exists or occurs with my awareness that *I* think the thought, he can plausibly be interpreted as distinguishing my mere introspective awareness of a thought from my experience of the thought as mine. So, what is it for me to have the sense that a thought is mine? One answer to this question is that for me to sense or experience a thought as *mine* is for me to recognize that I am the *subject* in whom, or in whose psychological history, the thought occurs. The issue here is distinguishing what occurs in me—within the "boundary of my ego"—from what occurs outside of me.

My sense that something occurs in me, within my ego boundary or psychological history, rather than outside me, is what we call my *sense of subjectivity*. Philosophers, psychologists, and other students of self-consciousness have long recognized that it is important for us as persons to distinguish what goes on within our mind or self from what goes on outside. They have speculated about how we manage to make this distinction correctly. They have discussed the possibility that we sometimes fail to make the distinction correctly. We might suffer "loss of ego boundaries" or "internal/external confusion," mislocating things internal to the self in the external environment or vice versa. Though this has been a point of controversy, it has seemed plausible to some theorists that mere introspective awareness of a thought might persist in the absence of the sense of subjectivity regarding the thought. If so, this would explain how I could be aware of my own thought and yet fail to recognize it as mine. Thus, it is tempting to believe that verbal hallucinations and thought insertion involve a split, as it were, between introspective awareness and the sense of subjectivity. Indeed, this account is suggested when these phenomena are conceptualized as loss of ego boundaries or as internal/external confusion.

We shall argue that neither verbal hallucination nor thought insertion is adequately explained on the loss-of-ego-boundary model. According to that model, subjects are introspectively aware of voices and inserted thoughts but have lost their sense that the relevant thoughts occur within themselves. The short answer as to why the model fails to account for the phenomena in question is that in both cases subjects clearly recognize that they are the subjects in whom the relevant alien episodes occur. That is to say, they correctly locate thoughts relative to their ego boundaries. Thus, the possibility that the sense of subjectivity might split off from introspection turns out to be irrelevant to the alienated self-experience involved in verbal hallucinations and thought insertion.

The possible contrast between introspection and the sense of subjectivity is the wrong conceptual distinction through which to understand thought insertion and verbal hallucination. But what else is involved in self-consciousness? What more could be involved in recognizing a thought as something that I think, than in having a sense of its subjectivity? Recall Fish's remark about the quality of my-ness connected with thought: "Thinking is experienced as an activity which is being *carried out* by the subject" (emphasis added). My sense that *I think* a certain thought involves more than the sense that the thought occurs in me. It also consists in a sense that I am author of that thought, that I carry out the activity of thinking. This sense of agency regarding my thinking is, we maintain, a normal component or strand in our experience of thinking. It is normally phenomenologically intertwined with introspective awareness as well as with the sense of subjectivity. However it is conceivable that self-consciousness should be disturbed and unravel in such a way that I retain my sense that I am the subject in whom a thought occurs but no longer have the sense that I am the agent who *thinks* or carries out the thought.

One might note that such a separation of the sense of subjectivity from the sense of agency would account for a way of experiencing my own thoughts that is more familiar and less alarming than verbal hallucination or thought insertion. Sometimes I feel passive with respect to my thoughts. I experience them as things that happen to me rather than as things that I do. However, this felt passivity could hardly explain the alien quality of some thought—i.e., my sense that it is someone else's thought. Consider, by analogy, the distinction (famous in philosophy) between my arm's going up and my raising my arm. I might have the sense that my arm has gone up without my raising it. However, this is certainly not the same as my thinking that someone else raised my arm. Meanwhile, it is possible for my arm to go up because somebody else raised it. Another person might be the agent who caused my arm to go up, in which case raising my arm would be his action rather than mine. It would be something that he carries out.

In the real world, an agent who raises someone else's arm is likely to accomplish the feat by such unsophisticated means as grasping the other's wrist and lifting. Still it is conceivable that the agent may employ more covert methods, such as applying electrical stimulation to the person's muscles or brain. Notoriously, there are people who entertain delusions to the effect that the movements of their body are controlled by agents employing similar or even more mysterious means. We suggest that one might likewise have the impression that another agent controls the "movements" of one's mind: that thoughts occur in one's mind through another's agency. Another person is the author of such thoughts, and they are, accordingly, his thoughts rather than one's own. Something like this is how we believe subjects experience alien thoughts in delusions of thought insertion and in at least some cases usually described as verbal hallucination.

Obviously this hypothesis requires stage setting and explanatory detail. We need to make the case that the sense of agency is a distinctive element in self-consciousness. Making that case requires us to confront various objections raised by philosophers to the very idea that thinking can be considered an intentional activity or action. We then need to make the case that the sense of agency is at issue in verbal hallucination and thought insertion. Our case will require arguing that delusions of thought insertion are, in some respects, less bizarre and more coherent than they otherwise appear. It also requires, for reasons which will be discussed, arguing that verbal hallucinations are a stranger and less readily comprehensible phenomenon than the standard account in the psychopathology literature might lead one to expect. Indeed, we shall argue that at least a substantial percentage of what are called verbal hallucinations aren't really hallucinatory in the usual understanding of that term. Many persons who are said to believe that they hear voices really don't believe that they *hear* voices at all. This is true even of people who are firmly convinced that the voices are alien and represent communication from another agent. We also will need to say something about just what the sense of agency *is*—i.e., what it is to experience oneself as the agent or author of thoughts. And we will take a stab, however speculative and tentative, at explaining how a subject could arrive at the conviction—no matter how delusory—that somebody else is doing his thinking in the subject's head.

We shall attempt all of the above in the context of a critical examination of verbal hallucinations and delusions of thought insertion, as these phenomena are understood in the contemporary literature on psychopathology. We want to do justice to the clinical facts (as we can best make them out) and to the most interesting theoretical approaches to explaining them.

If nothing else, we want this book to serve as a useful guide to some of the work that is being done in psychiatry on verbal hallucinations and thought insertion. We will also consider what philosophers have had to say about the issues that arise in the course of our discussion of verbal hallucinations and inserted thoughts.

In recent years, work by philosophically informed clinicians and mental health professionals and by philosophers sensitive to clinical data has shown how philosophical psychology can illuminate and be illuminated by the study of psychopathology.[4] We

4. Some philosophically informed clinicians and mental health professionals: Eagle (1988), Frith (1992), Fulford (1989), Gillett (1986, 1991), Hoffman (1986), Sass (1992). Some philosophers sensitive to clinical data: Braude (1995), P. S. Churchland (1983), Dennett (1991), Flanagan (1992), Radden (1996), Wilkes (1988). Our intellectual debts to these and other authors go substantially beyond what is indicated in specific citations in the text. For a fuller discussion of work at the intersection of psychiatry and philosophical psychology, see Graham and Stephens 1994.

hope to contribute to this ongoing interchange. We believe that a critical, "philosophical" examination of the clinical literature on verbal hallucinations and thought insertion will yield a more precise understanding of the alienated experience of self involved in these phenomena. Understanding how self-consciousness breaks or is disturbed when we hear voices and confront alien thoughts will give us some empirical leverage on the question of how self-consciousness works.

2

Voice Lessons

The voices that so continually and insistently plague many schizophrenics have long tantalized students of the disordered mind. That they are generated in the patient's own mind (brain) one can hardly doubt.—Marcel Kinsbourne (1990)

2.1 Conceiving Voices

Your inner speech is your own. My inner speech is my own.

Our inner speech is our own, but we do not always experience it as our own. We sometimes experience our inner speech as the voice of another person. We "hear voices." Somehow we fail to recognize our own inner speech as our own. The question, of course, is "Why?" If a voice really is a person's own voice, why does he fail to perceive it as his own and how can one hear one's own speech as the speech of another?

Let us begin with an illustration adapted from P. D. Slade and R. P. Bentall's book *Sensory Deception* (1988). A young man—call him Jesse—complains that he is the victim of a "thought-control" experiment. A team of "parapsychologists" plants voices in his head. Among other things he frequently hears the message "Give cancer to the crippled bastard." Questioned by his doctor, Jesse admits that the voices may be products of his imagination, but he insists that this is unlikely "because of their vividness and content." Slade and Bentall remark that the patient's mother had died of cancer and that he walked with a pronounced limp due to injuries suffered in a suicide attempt (p. 3).

Experiences like Jesse's are classified by clinicians as "voices," "verbal hallucinations," and sometimes as "auditory hallucinations," although this last expression sometimes also covers hallucinations of non-speech sounds. Some patients find it difficult to make out what their voices are saying. Usually, though, they report the very words and even the manner (sneeringly, consolingly, threateningly, and so on) in which the voice conveys its message. Subjects typically also report that the voice addresses them directly or makes special reference to them. They regard the message as salient to their person or circumstances.

Voices figure conspicuously in the symptomatology of a major form of mental illness: schizophrenia (American Psychiatric Association 1994, p. 275). Their connection with schizophrenia explains the proprietary interest in voices among mental health professionals and provides the context for most clinical and experimental studies of verbal hallucinations. Indeed, investigators often fault accounts of voices for failing to relate them to the underlying pathology of schizophrenia (Kinsbourne 1990, p. 811). However, it is now generally acknowledged that verbal hallucinations also occur in non-schizophrenic mental disorders, including alcoholic hallucinosis and manic-depressive psychosis (bipolar disorder), as well as in certain organic conditions, e.g. temporal lobe epilepsy, neurosyphilis, and Wilson's disease. (See Slade and Bentall 1988, p. 39; McKenna 1994, p. 282; Coleman and Gillberg 1996, pp. 75–76, 134–136, 250.) There are, likewise, credible reports of voices occurring in people who do not suffer from diagnosed illness. W. D. Reese's study of verbal hallucinations in widows and widowers (1971) and Posey and Losch (1983), who found that 70 percent of a fairly large sample of college students admitted to having experienced voices on at least one occasion, are two cases in point.

As philosophers, with proprietary interests of our own, we would be loath to admit a necessary connection between voices and mental illness. After all, Socrates heads the list of prominent historical figures reported to have heard them:

It may seem strange to you that . . . I do not venture to go to the assembly and there advise the city. You have heard me give the reason for this in many places. I have a divine sign from the god. . . . This began when I was a child. It is a voice, and whenever it speaks it turns me away from something I am about to do. . . . This is what has prevented me from taking part in public affairs. (Apology 31d, Plato (1981))

Thus, we feel compelled to echo the sentiments of the Dutch historian Johan Huizinga (1959, p. 222) who, commenting on another famous case of voices, remarked:

Indeed, if every inspiration that comes to one with such commanding urgency that it is heard as a voice is to be condemned out of hand (as a morbid symptom . . . who would not rather stand with Joan of Arc and Socrates on the side of the mad than with the faculty of the Sorbonne on the side of the sane.

In any event, this is a book about verbal hallucinations (and certain other particular experiences of breakdown in self-consciousness), not about schizophrenia. We shall take our examples of voices where we find them. We hope to illuminate some general features of human self-experience rather than the specific pathology of schizophrenia.

Jesse reports hearing a voice, not his own, saying "Give cancer to the crippled bastard." Of course, having the sense that another is saying something is not an unusual human experience. Normally this experience is easily explained: another *is* saying something. What initially attracts attention to voices, however, and warrants classifying them as hallucinations, is that they occur in the absence of remotely appropriate environmental stimuli. Outsiders do not observe anyone talking to the subject when he experiences the voice. The subject may attempt to explain away this discrepancy by supposing that the speaker has special powers or means of communicating with him. Mental health professionals typically discount such explanations.

Less bizarre, the subject may have overheard another saying "Give cancer to the crippled bastard" but may mistakenly believe that the speech was directed at him. Such phenomena, called *delusions of reference*, also occur in schizophrenia. However, few reports of voices can be classified as delusions of reference. This is because the subject's experience of voices typically does not depend on actually hearing another speak. Indeed, it is not unusual for subjects to report hearing voices even when they know that no one else really is talking to them. Knowledge of its hallucinatory character rarely silences the voice.

Given that Jesse does not hear someone else say "Give cancer to the crippled bastard," what explains his sense that he does? The explanation that comes most readily to mind is that he somehow says "Give cancer to the crippled bastard" to himself, but that he experiences the speech activity as another's voice. As Marcel Kinsbourne crisply puts it (1990, p. 811), "one can hardly doubt" that the subject himself "generates" the voice. But the subject fails to recognize, or at least to acknowledge, that it originates in himself.

"[He] is talking to himself but perceives the voice as coming from somewhere else." (Frith 1992, p. 71)

This conception of voices, which we shall call the *self-produced but misattributed* (SPM) conception, is widely endorsed in the clinical literature. A few citations suggest its popularity:

The voices are strictly the patient's own thoughts which he has chosen, presumably without conscious awareness, to project onto the outside world. (Snyder 1974, p. 121)

. . . auditory verbal hallucinations are related to the psychotic patient's own verbal thoughts. . . . They arise when verbal thoughts are misrecognized as being of alien (non-self) origin and are thus perceived as external "voices." (McGuire et al. 1996, p. 148)

Thomas Szasz offers a variation on SPM. He dismisses the notion that voices are symptoms of mental pathology, but he takes it as obvious that when psychiatrists talk about voices they refer to cases in which people talk to themselves. "Today," Szasz remarks (1996, p. 5),

self-conversation is regarded as a symptom of an abnormal and dangerous mental state and is called "hearing voices."

Disagreements over the presence of pathology notwithstanding, each of the above theorists shares a common conception of voices. Each endorses the twin assumptions of the SPM conception: (i) that subjects generate or produce the message expressed by the voice and (ii) that they misattribute the voice to another person or agent. Each endorses SP; each embraces M.

The first (SP) assumption of self-production is virtually unavoidable. Given the absence of appropriate outside stimuli, we must allow that the subject's impression that he hears a voice saying "Give cancer to the crippled bastard" is determined by factors internal to the subject. Events within him, rather than occurrences in the external environment, somehow must account for why he hears a voice uttering certain words and in a certain manner. In articulating this SP assumption, the SPM conception supposes, in addition, that the subject self-produces a *verbal* message. Voices are organized in words or "verbal thoughts." Thus, the events in a subject that explain why he takes himself to hear a voice are commonly referred to as *inner speech*. Reference to inner speech helps to explain the verbal quality of a voice.

Of course, where the subject of voices goes wrong, or at least where his impression is misleading, is in the subject's sense that the voice is of alien or external origin—that it comes from someone other than himself. This is the M of the SPM conception. Subjects of voices misattribute their own inner speech to another person or agent.

2.2　What Is Inner Speech?

Proponents of the SPM conception presume that the subject produces the message he hears in "inner speech," "verbal thoughts," or "verbal imagery," rather than speaking the words aloud. The reason for this assumption is simply that, just as observers do not hear anyone else speak to the subject, they do not hear the subject talk to himself. The message appears accessible only to the subject. Thus, it is classified as speech but also as inner rather than outer speech.

The inner-speech hypothesis is natural enough. Inner speech—our ability to "talk" silently to ourselves—occupies an important place in our folk-psychological or common-sense account of our mental life. Inner speech paradigmatically exemplifies the process of thinking and has done so for some time, as the following passage from Plato's *Theatetus* (1961, pp. 895–896) makes clear.

Socrates: And do you accept my description of the process of thinking?
Theatetus: How do you describe it?
Socrates: As a discourse that the mind carries on with itself. . . . I have the notion that, when the mind is thinking, it is simply talking to itself, asking questions and answering them. . . . So I should describe thinking as discourse and a judgment as a statement pronounced, not aloud to someone else, but silently to oneself.

Likewise, the contribution of inner speech to phenomena other than verbal hallucination (such as memory) has been studied by psychologists and neurologists (Baddeley 1986). Even philosophical behaviorists sometimes refer to inner speech without embarrassment. Here is Gilbert Ryle (1949, p. 169):

I learn that a certain pupil of mine is lazy, ambitious, and witty by following his work, noticing his excuses, listening to his conversation. . . . Nor does it make any important difference if I happen myself to be that pupil. I can indeed listen to more of his conversations, as I am the addressee of his unspoken soliloquies.

But should we embrace the hypothesis that voices are due to *inner* speech: to *silent* soliloquies? The worry here is that formulating the SPM conception in terms of something inner or silent invites objections against the SPM conception of the sort that have been raised against appeals to inner or private events in other explanations of psychological phenomena. Philosophers refer to these as "metaphysical" or "ontological" objections. Frank Jackson once defended the existence of private events in a hotly contested paper on the topic of phenomenal consciousness, all the while conceding that they are a "total mystery" and "an excrescence" (1982, p. 135). To many theorists, Jackson included, there is only a thin line between invoking inner or private events and throwing up one's hands in conceptual despair.[1]

Of course there is room for debate over whether pessimistic fears about the metaphysical acceptability of reference to private events is justified. However, in this book, rather than recapitulate debates over privacy and ontology or metaphysics, we prefer to discuss whether there is a genuine explanatory need to suppose, as is assumed by the SPM conception, that inner (private) speech plays a role in voices. We try to bring out issues about inner speech in a way that is more directly relevant to the problem of explaining verbal hallucinations than to the controversy about privacy.

Furthermore, it is one thing to worry, in a pessimistic ontic vein, whether we can or should refer to inner speech; it is another to specify explanatory alternatives to reference to inner speech. Each of the alternatives discussed in the literature on voices has its own distinctive features and raises its own distinctive problems. There isn't enough space here to consider all the alternatives that have been proposed, but let us examine one briefly. This examination will help us to suggest why invoking "inner speech" to explain the verbal quality of voices appears as the most promising option.

2.3   Mouths Wide Open

One theoretical alternative to referring to private or inner speech to account for the verbal quality of voices is that this quality is due to low-volume (subvocal and thus not naturally audible) but potentially audible speech—i.e., that voices are whispers or subvocalizations. (Some theorists refer to subvocal or whispered

1. See also Jackson 1998, p. 101.

speech as "inner" speech, although we do not follow this stipulation here. The stipulation confuses the terminological terrain. Whispering isn't inner any more than secretly putting pennies in your pocket makes them inner. (Mentally pictured pennies may be inner, but pennies in a pocket are not.) Let us call this the *whisper hypothesis*. If the whisper hypothesis is correct, hallucinators actually hear, not just "hear," their voices, and with suitable technological assistance outside observers may actually hear them too.

Louis Gould, a psychiatrist, noted that one of his patients seemed to whisper to herself when she heard voices. Using a microphone, Gould amplified her indistinct subvocalizations and was able to make out what she was saying and to correlate its contents with her reports of what the voices said to her. In a paper published in the *Journal of Nervous and Mental Disease* in 1949, Gould reported the following:

The subvocal speech continued, "She knows. She's the most wicked thing in the whole, wide world. She knows everything. She knows all about aviation." At this point [the patient] stated audibly: "I heard them say that I have a knowledge of aviation."

More recently, Green and Preston (1981) employed auditory feedback to induce a hallucinating patient to gradually increase the volume of his subvocal speech until he was engaged in a fully audible conversation with his voice.

Bick and Kinsbourne (1987) reviewed several additional reports of hallucinating subjects' whispered speech. Their findings have been greeted with surprise (McKenna 1994, p. 175) and skepticism (Frith 1992, p. 72), suggesting that they may not reflect typical clinical experience. Reviewing the evidence, Slade and Bentall (1988, pp. 126–131) find some reason to accept that there is a general connection between subvocalization and inner speech, and they find stronger support for a link between subvocalization and verbal hallucinations. However, they understand "subvocalization" to include a wide range of neurological and muscular activities that need not involve the production of audible speech sounds. Kinsbourne (1990, p. 811) characterizes the published work on the whisper hypothesis as "sparse and spotty" and complains that much of it was "inadequately controlled." He concludes, nevertheless, that the evidence favors the hypothesis "on balance."

Would that the hypothesis were true. If subjects produced their voices in whispered speech, then students of verbal hallucination, equipped with suitable technology, could ascertain their occurrence and their content without relying on the subjects' reports. Advocates of the SPM conception could eschew reference to private events or "inner" speech in their accounts of voices. Subjects would be *talking* to themselves and *listening* to their own speech in the most literal sense. Proponents of the SPM conception could then devote themselves, with a clear metaphysical conscience, to the task of explaining why hallucinators misattribute their own whispered speech to another speaker.

However, Kinsbourne and his collaborators call attention to a persistent failing of studies supporting the hypothesis that voices represent the subject's low-volume speech. Even if these studies establish a correlation between voices and subvocal speech, they do "not prove that the voices are actually the patient's own speech sounds" (Bick and Kinsbourne 1987, p. 223). Subvocalizations might be "causally irrelevant sequelae," accompanying or "shadowing" the subject's experience of the voice (ibid., p. 222). Perhaps the subject first "hears" the voice (in inner speech) and then repeats (shadows) its message in whispered speech acts. In order to rule out this possibility, advocates of the whisper hypothesis must show that the subject's hearing his own subvocal speech constitutes his experience of the voice. Kinsbourne addresses this problem in two papers, one written with Bick (Bick and Kinsbourne 1987) and one with Green (Green and Kinsbourne 1989). He reasons that if subvocal speech or whispering is the source of verbal hallucination then activities that interfere with the subject's ability to produce subvocal speech should block the occurrence of hallucination. If, on the other hand, subvocal speech merely shadows or repeats the voice (otherwise produced by inner speech), such interference should have no effect on hallucination.

In the study reported in Bick and Kinsbourne 1987, subjects prone to verbal hallucinations (including schizophrenic patients and student volunteers hallucinating in response to hypnotic suggestion) were instructed to hold their mouths wide open when they began to hallucinate. This task had been previously shown to inhibit subvocal speech. (In control trials subjects were instructed to make a fist or shut their eyes tight under the same conditions.) Bick and Kinsbourne found that 14 of the 18 schizophrenic subjects, and 18 of the 21 hypnotic subjects, reported that their voices "went away" when they held their mouths wide open. The control tasks were reported to abolish the voice in only two cases in each group. In no instance did a subject report that one of the control tasks was effective but that mouth opening was not. Bick and Kinsbourne (ibid., p. 223) conclude as follows:

The finding that obstructing subvocalization suppresses auditory hallucinations clarifies the mechanism by which these experiences are generated. The previously reported correlation between voices and subvocal activity did not identify cause and effect. The patient could have been repeating (shadowing) what he or she heard. . . . But were that so, the patient could not have inhibited the perceptual experience by otherwise engaging his or her vocal apparatus. We therefore infer the following sequence of events: The patient subvocalizes, listens to his or her covert speech, and attributes it to another.

In another study, Green and Kinsbourne (1989) found that softly humming a single note inhibited verbal hallucinations in 15 of 17 subjects. This finding is compatible with the conclusion of the earlier study, since humming occupies the vocal musculature and inhibits subvocalization. However, Green and Kinsbourne failed to reconfirm the effectiveness of holding the mouth open. In their 1989 study, that task showed no tendency to reduce hallucination. They remark that this failure might have been an artifact of the experimental design. Subjects in the 1989 study had electrodes attached to their mouths, and this may have prevented them from opening their mouths wide enough to prevent subvocalization. Subjects were also required to hold their mouths open for 90-second intervals, which they found difficult. Kinsbourne (1990, p. 811) says that, on balance, the evidence provided in Bick and Kinsbourne 1987 and in Green and Kinsbourne 1989 favors the hypothesis that subvocal speech is the source of rather than a causally irrelevant sequel to the hallucinated experience.

The studies recounted above provide limited but fairly impressive evidence that blocking subvocalization blocks verbal hallucinations. However, this evidence does not establish that a subject's *auditory perception* of subvocal speech constitutes his experience of voices. Recall Bick and Kinsbourne's three-step account of what happens in verbal hallucinations: "The patient subvocalizes, *listens to his or her covert speech*, and attributes it to another." (1987, p. 223, emphasis added) It may be that subvocalization is necessary for the occurrence of verbal hallucinations but that hearing sounds produced by subvocal activities is not. Perhaps subjects experience the physiological activities involved in subvocalization as inner speech or verbal imagery but do not actually hear anything.

Whether auditory perception plays a crucial role in experiences of voices could be experimentally investigated by studies similar in design to those carried out by Bick, Green, and Kinsbourne. One would need to determine whether blocking a subject's auditory perception of sounds produced by subvocalization also blocks his experience of voices. Though we are not aware that any such studies have been attempted, there is reason to doubt that auditory perception of subvocal speech is necessary for verbal hallucinations. McGuire et al. (1996) found no distinctive audible output from subjects performing a variety of inner-speech tasks. This suggests that subvocalization need not involve production of speech sounds. However, McGuire et al. did not investigate subvocalizations associated with voices. In addition, as we shall discuss in chapter 4, there is solid evidence that profoundly deaf subjects can experience verbal hallucinations. Apparently, people can "hear" voices without being able to actually hear anything at all.

In light of the problems raised above, we are skeptical about the whisper hypothesis. Some hallucinators may well be articulating in subvocal speech the messages expressed by their voices. It seems doubtful, however, that auditory perceptions of such subvocal mutterings lie at the source of all or most experiences of voices. We should also note that Kinsbourne's most recent work on the whisper hypothesis (1990) introduces subtle refinements which, on our reading, raise questions about whether he remains committed to the claim that hallucinators are literally hearing themselves speak.

Voices are commonly taken to be a species of auditory hallucinations. According to the dominant stereotype, subjects feel as if they are hearing someone speak. The experience of the voice

seems auditory. The whisper hypothesis provides a natural explanation of this phenomenology. Voices seem auditory because they
arise from genuine auditory perceptions. In chapter 5 we shall
argue that the dominant stereotype misrepresents the phenomenology of voices. Voices are not, in general, auditory hallucinations. In many cases, subjects experiencing verbal hallucinations
do not have the impression that they are *hearing* voices. Thus,
when one accurately describes the phenomenology of voices, the
whisper hypothesis loses much of its natural appeal.

2.4   Fast Confabulation

In *The Cognitive Neuropsychology of Schizophrenia* (1992), Christopher Frith, although sympathetic to the misattribution (M)
assumption of the SPM conception, says that "it is unlikely that
all (verbal) hallucinations in schizophrenia are based on . . .
speech" and that "the basic experience underlying many so-called
auditory hallucinations is occurring at a more abstract level in
which there is no sensory component" (p. 77). Elsewhere in the
same book, Frith suggests that the subject's experience may be,
sometimes, more a matter of receiving information than a matter
of hearing a voice (p. 73). To support this observation, he cites a
study by Alpert and Silvers (1970) comparing verbal hallucinations reported by schizophrenics and those reported by alcoholics.
Alpert and Silvers found that alcoholics were more likely to
mention specific "sensory" features of the voice, such as its apparent volume or pitch, whereas "hallucinations of schizophrenics
have a more cognitive taint, appearing more like thoughts that
have become audible."

Later we shall offer our own explanation of the "nonsensory" (nonphenomenal, nonauditory) character of some voices.

For the nonce, let us briefly consider the following possibility: Suppose that a person finds himself with the "information" that someone is trying to kill him. He has no initial sense of how he acquired this information, but he is surprised to have it. He doesn't recall thinking of it previously or having been engaged in inquiry or rumination that might have caused it to come to mind. He thinks "It is as if I happened to overhear someone say something." Perhaps, he hypothesizes, "Someone *must* have said something to me." Asked by his psychiatrist if he ever "hears voices," he responds "Yes, I heard a voice saying 'Kill the bastard.'"

Why couldn't something like the above story be true for all instances of verbal hallucinations? There is nothing experiential, nothing audition-like, in the voices. Why suppose that subjects ever have any experience of voices? Why assume that awareness of some subjectively experienced speech act or episode of inner speech plays any role in the subject's coming to report that he hears a voice? Couldn't reports of voices simply be *ex post facto* explanations, sincere confabulations, of how the subject comes to acquire certain information?

Most reports of voices are nothing like the vague, hypothetical story told above. Subjects typically have a firm and precise idea as to when they acquired the "information" expressed by the voice. They claim to hear voices on specific occasions in specific experiences over definite periods of time. Often, in experimental and clinical settings, a subject claims to be hearing voices as he speaks to the interviewer. Further, subjects report not just acquiring information to the effect that, e.g. someone is trying to kill them. Rather, they insist that a voice uttered certain words and uttered them in a certain manner (e.g., harshly or mockingly). Often they describe the voice as male or female. For example, the patient Green and Preston (1981) found to be talking subvocally to himself claimed that he was hearing a woman's voice. How is one to explain the subjects' definite impressions concerning the timing, verbal content, and other characteristics of a voice unless one supposes that these impressions have a basis in their conscious experience: that subjects were aware of an episode that seemed to exhibit the relevant characteristics of the voice. Moreover, since in the case of voices, we know that subjects don't perceive someone else's speech, then they must produce the relevant experience themselves. They must have spoken to themselves "internally."

The above remarks make a case for saying that some sort of experience of inner speech occurs in subjects who report hearing voices. However, the philosopher Daniel Dennett might offer an alternative explanation. The following story is suggested by Dennett's account in *Consciousness Explained* (1991):

A person finds herself possessed of certain information. She supposes that she must somehow have acquired this information, so she tells a tale about how she acquired it. This story, of which she herself is sincerely convinced, is reflected in her introspective reports. She says, for instance, that she heard someone express the information to her. Realizing that if she heard it, she must have heard it at a particular time, she elaborates this story so as to specify the time-frame. Recognizing that if someone said it to her, they must have spoken in a certain manner, she adds description of the speaker's tone and style of delivery. Since the speaker must have been male or female, she specifies the speaker's sex. She produces this account rapidly and effortlessly, convincing herself and, perhaps, other observers that she has had a vivid, richly detailed conscious experience of a voice.

It is one thing to commit, in a general way, to the notion that subjects of voices experience their own inner speech which they misattribute to external agencies. It is another to try to "explain" (away) these experiences as confabulations, rapidly composed if sincerely endorsed avowals designed to account for why certain information (e.g. someone wants to kill me) occurs to a person.

Who is right here: the SPM conception, or Dennett? Flanagan (1992) has discussed the distinction between (i) describing psychological episodes as occurring independent of subjects' beliefs about them (and thus being distinguishable from *ex post facto* fast confabulation, however sincere) and (ii) describing them as a kind of "user illusion" created by a subject's beliefs about the origin of information. Block (1993) and others charge that Dennett's tale of fast confabulation is a theoretical muddle blurring his field of philosophical vision. However, Dennett would insist that no empirical or clinical evidence could give us reason to prefer the I-heard-a-voice experience postulated by the SPM conception over his own confabulatory explanation. The subject of voices insists that she was vividly aware of something speech-like. She insists that she had conscious *experience* of a voice. But this is just what we should expect a sincere confabulator to claim!

Since Dennett insists that we have no empirically decisive way to distinguish between a person's really having had certain experiences and a person's forming certain beliefs about those experiences, it is, therefore, otiose, according to him, to appeal to "inner experience"—to verbal imagery—in psychological explanations of beliefs about experience; postulating private speech or verbal imagery to serve as a source for the subject's convictions about voices gets us nowhere.

We don't propose a direct frontal assault on Dennettonian skepticism about hallucinatory experience (or phenomenal consciousness in general). To avoid that sort of metaphysical quarrel, our approach to voices (and to alienated self-consciousness more generally) is ontologically agnostic. We assume that the SPM conception of voices can be developed and defended without taking a stand on the wisdom of any position (like Dennett's) concerning the ultimate unreality of verbal imagery or the ultimate nature of inner speech. The SPM conception assumes that people really can and do engage in inner speech and that a subject's undergoing verbal hallucinations consists in his having an alienated (i.e., misattributed) experience of his own inner speech. Inner speech is, roughly, *whatever* it is that people are doing when they engage in inner-speech tasks or activities—when, for example, one silently recites a poem, rehearses an argument, or debates with oneself over a choice. Reference to verbal imagery is a way of identifying how producing inner speech appears to its subject. It is a way of describing what it is like to silently recite a poem, rehearse an argument, and so on. Perhaps such descriptions need not involve commitment to the existence of voice experiences which are independent of beliefs (confabulated or otherwise) about them. It may be (although we think not) that generating inner speech just is a matter of a subject's forming beliefs in the manner suggested by Dennett. Or perhaps, *pace* Dennett, inner speech involves awareness of purely experiential characteristics (such as verbal auditory imagery).

In any case, the key methodological point is that subjects themselves firmly believe that there is more to hearing voices than merely acquiring information and telling a story about it. They are convinced that they somehow experience speech or specific verbally encoded messages delivered in a certain manner. Thus, any explanation of verbal hallucination must include an account of this aspect of the phenomenon, which we call its *apparent verbal quality*. The hypothesis that subjects are aware of self-generated inner speech provides an explanation of the verbal quality of voices that is plausible in light of what they themselves say or believe about how voices seem to them.

Ours will be an account of voices as subjects interpret them to themselves and report them to outside observers. Our reference point for what voices are like is what people who are supposed to hear them say about them. We take this point of view critically and reflectively. It may involve challenging or explaining away bits and pieces of what people say about voices in the interest of developing a coherent account. However, the account operates within the limits and constraints of the clinically presented picture. From our clinically respectful point of view, we are perfectly willing to allow that distinctions built into subjects' reports (such as the independence of voice experiences from *ex post facto* beliefs about them), may not reflect deep truths, and that there may be large-scale metaphysical worries about voices (for example, concerning the privacy of inner speech) to which the perspective is oblivious. However, these distinctively philosophical issues seem only to offer greater scope for explanatory contestability. Sticking to the clinical locality of reports clears the way for an explanation of voices, metaphysical contest notwithstanding.

3

The Auditory-Hallucination Model of Voices

3.1 The Prospect of a Theory

In this chapter we introduce a general approach to explaining the alien quality of voices. This quality is the reference of M in the SPM conception of voices mentioned in chapter 2.

The general approach begins with the assumption that voices are auditory hallucinations and attempts to explain the alien character of voices by reference to their apparent auditory character or quality. For this reason, we refer to this approach as the *auditory-hallucination model* (AHM).

The overall strategy for accounting for the alien quality of voices incorporated in the AHM is as follows: The subject's experience of his own inner speech when he "hears" voices is very similar to his typical experience of hearing another person speak. Because of this similarity between voices and genuine auditory perception, subjects are prone to mistake experiences of voices for experiences of genuine auditory perception of another's speech. This is what the alien quality of voices consists in: the subject confuses his introspective or imagistic experience of his own speech with a perceptual experience of someone else's speech. Thus, in verbal hallucinations we confront an instance of the general problem of distinguishing what we imagine from what we really perceive.

As sketched above, the AHM may seem as empty as it is obvious.

Obvious? It seems only to clarify what is implicit in the standard terminology for referring to voices. Voices are classified as hallucinations, so of course they "resemble" corresponding perceptual experiences.

What about emptiness? The attempt to explain why the subject mistakes hallucinations for perceptual experiences in terms of supposed similarities threatens to turn back on itself. How can the similarities be described without appealing to the notion that one sort of experience is mistaken for, and hence is similar to, the other?

Despite these reservations, it is worth attending to the AHM. First, whether obvious or not, the AHM is something like the received view of the alien quality of voices in the literature. It is accepted by Slade and Bentall (1988), Kinsbourne (1990), Hoffman (1986), and (with some qualifications) Frith (1992)— the researchers whose work on voices we find the most detailed and helpful. Second, although general appeal to similarities between hallucinating and perceptual experiences does little by itself to explain why subjects mistake voices for auditory perception, particular versions of the AHM—particular forms of such appeal—developed by the above authors and others involve specific proposals regarding the nature of the relevant similarities between voices and auditory perceptions. These authors are careful to guard against charges of emptiness or circularity.

The AHM should be thought of as a family of explanations. All members share the notions that (i) subjects who experience verbal hallucinations take themselves to be perceiving a voice and (ii) this mistake or impression plays a crucial role in explaining the alien quality of voices. However, within these constraints there is considerable room for theoretical variation. Differences in specifics are significant. In the next chapter we will begin to examine one version of the AHM in considerable detail, and we will indicate how it differs from other versions of the AHM model. The present chapter is devoted to a general discussion of the AHM.

We have one further reason for devoting a whole chapter to a general discussion of the AHM. We claim that, at best, a version of the AHM could explain the alien character merely of *some* experiences labeled as "voices" or "verbal hallucinations." Often, people who "hear" voices do not have the impression that they are *hearing.* Voices are not, in general, experienced as audition-like.[1] Even when voices involve auditory hallucination, one may plausibly question whether their auditory or audition-like character explains their alien quality. In any case, we shall offer a very different approach to explaining the alien quality of voices than that of the AHM. By first developing the AHM as our main competitor, we hope to make clear the distinctive features of our own approach.

3.2   Hallucination and Perception

Subjects who hear voices are engaged in inner speech but fail to recognize the self-produced character of their inner speech. They silently talk to themselves, in some sense, although they have the impression that someone else is doing the talking. There is, of

---

1. This claim is shared by Christopher Frith (1992), who accepts an AHM account of the alien quality of only those voices that are auditory.

course, nothing pathological or strange about talking to yourself. People do it all the time. But we do not typically experience our inner speech as messages from external agencies.[2] Frith (1992, p. 73) remarks:

If hallucinations are caused by inner speech, then the problem is not that inner speech is occurring, but that patients must be failing to recognize that this activity is self-initiated. The patients misattribute self-generated actions to external agents.

Thus, the proposal that voices originate in inner speech does nothing to explain their alien quality. Indeed, it seems to make the problem of accounting for their external character more acute, since inner speech is self-generated and subjects presumably are intimately familiar with the experience of their own inner speech. It is, therefore, understandable that researchers who accept the view that voices originate in the subject's experience of inner speech, as does Ralph Hoffman, regard the problem of explaining the alien quality of verbal hallucinations as the central task of a theory of voices. Hoffman (1986, p. 504) writes:

[Verbal hallucinations] are instances of auditory imagery that are phonetically organized as words. Verbal images are a normal component of human consciousness. . . . This immediately raises the central issue . . . : What specific factors lead schizophrenic persons to experience certain images of verbal imagery as if they were actually coming from another person.

It may seem, as we noted earlier, that an explanation of the alien quality of voices is implicit in the standard terminology used

2. At least not any more. In *The Origin of Consciousness and the Breakdown of the Bicameral Mind* (1976), Julian Jaynes argues that in the ancient world people did standardly experience their inner speech as alien. In Jaynes's speculation, verbal hallucinations are a vestige of an earlier developmental stage of human self-consciousness.

to describe them. Voices are spoken of as auditory or verbal *hallucinations*.

Slade and Bentall, who offer an extensive and careful discussion of hallucinatory experiences, define 'hallucination' as follows (1988, p. 23):

any percept-like experience which (a) occurs in the absence of an appropriate stimulus, (b) has the full force and impact of the corresponding actual (real) perception, and (c) is not amenable to direct or voluntary control by the experiencer.

Their account emphasizes common features of hallucination and "the corresponding actual perception" (clauses b and c). Hallucinations and perceptions apparently are distinguished only by their respective etiologies: the causal connection or lack of such connection to "an appropriate stimulus" (clause a).

How does characterizing voices as hallucinations help to explain their alien quality? Here again are Slade and Bentall (ibid., p. 205):

There is a fundamental assumption about the nature of hallucinations that all theories have in common: that hallucinators mistake their own, internal, mental, or private events for external or publicly observable events.

Thus, the hallucinator takes what is in fact an episode occurring within his own mind to be something occurring external to him (i.e., belonging to the outside world). The apparent externality of what is internal is what the alien quality of hallucinations amounts to.

Actually, the above way of putting things seems epistemically uncharitable to the hallucinator. No doubt, hallucinators have the impression that certain things exist in their external environments that cannot really be found there—e.g., a pink elephant, or some person who is speaking. But is it really accurate to claim that these misimpressions involve the subject's somehow taking one of his own *mental* activities to be occurring outside him? A more charitable reading is that the subject mistakes one sort of mental event or activity for another. Specifically, he mistakes an "imaginative" or merely introspective experience for a perceptual one. Since a defining characteristic of perceptions is that they presuppose the existence of external objects, the subject's taking an imaginative experience to be perceptual explains his mistaken beliefs about what exists in his external environment.

Further, in view of the subjective similarity between hallucinations and their corresponding perceptions, we seem to have a ready story to tell about why subjects mistake hallucinations for perceptions. In any case where a person mistakes one sort of thing for another (e.g., a decoy for a duck, or a forged Goya for a real one), the mistake is understandable if the two things are similar.

How does all this apply to voices and to the AHM? Voices, we have assumed here in explicating the AHM picture, are a subspecies of hallucination. They are "auditory verbal hallucinations"; that is, they involve hallucinations of speech sounds. Their "corresponding actual perceptions" are auditory perceptions of speech. The subject is introspectively aware of his own inner speech or verbal imagery, but he mistakes this experience for auditory perception of speech. The subject's hallucinatory experience of a voice saying "Give cancer to the crippled bastard," for example, resembles, and hence is readily mistaken for, an auditory perception of someone speaking these words.

In fact the assumption that the subject takes himself to be hearing the voice still does not yet explain the alien quality of voices. A subject could take himself to be hearing his own voice (as happens when people listen to themselves delivering a speech or whispering in a theatre). Interestingly, there is another sort of hallucinatory experience associated with schizophrenia, called *Gedankenlautwerden*, in which subjects report hearing their own thoughts spoken aloud.[3] In such cases, the apparently audible character of the thoughts does not lead the subject to deny that they are his own.

Thus, there must be more to the story of why subjects regard voices as alien than merely that they take themselves to be hearing the voice. A number of possibilities suggest themselves. For example, hearing oneself speak is normally a qualitatively different experience from hearing someone else speak. This is true because some of our perception of our own speech comes to us via bone conduction and because auditory perception involves an impression of the spatial location of the sound source relative to the perceiver (Hoffman 1986, pp. 537–538). So perhaps hallucinatory voices sound more like hearing someone else talk than they sound like hearing yourself talk.

Alternatively, when I am speaking audibly this activity is accompanied by muscular and kinesthetic sensations produced by my own vocal movements. When I hear another person speak I get no kinesthetic feedback. Thus, I might distinguish instances in which I hear my own voice from instances in which I hear another's voice by noting the presence or absence of the relevant kinesthetic sensations. Supposing that my production of inner speech is not accompanied by the movements of my vocal

3. We are unable to discover in the literature whether such subjects typically report that they "hear" their thoughts spoken aloud in their own voice or in the voice of another. The latter sometimes is the case: see Sims 1995, pp. 149–151.

musculature typically involved in overt speech production, then my experience of my inner speech might be kinesthetically more similar to hearing another speak than to hearing myself speak. Thus, if I have a vivid, apparently auditory experience of my own inner speech, I might mistake it for a genuine auditory perception of another's speech due to lack of accompanying kinesthetic feedback. Even on the assumption that production of inner speech does involve activity in the vocal musculature, such activity might be too subtle to create kinesthetic sensations typical of overt speech production.

The supposition that the subject takes himself to hear the voice is not the whole story about the alien quality of the voices, even according to the AHM picture, but it may be a crucial part of the story.

3.3 Reality Discrimination

It is easy to characterize the experience of verbal hallucination as it is understood in the AHM. In contrast to some of the more bizarre manifestations of psychopathology and neuropathology (for example, the delusion that one does not exist), which are hard to imagine, we can readily imagine what it is like to hear voices: it's like hearing someone else talk. One is tempted to add "and that's why it's called *hearing* voices."

However, we should avoid reading too much phenomenological commitment into reference to "hearing" voices. Everyone, including clinicians, patients and members of the general public, uses the expression "hearing voices" to describe experiences of verbal hallucination. This does not necessarily mean that the experience of voices is extremely similar to, or is likely to be mistaken for the experience of, auditory speech perception.

Terminology can be misleading. For example, people standardly speak of *seeing* mental images when describing what they do when they try to imagine or recall some object or event. This does not indicate that they regard imagining a pink elephant as very similar to the experience of visually perceiving a pink elephant, or that they would agree that the two experiences can be readily confused. On the contrary, they typically contrast the experience of imagining a pink elephant with the much more vivid and forceful experience of actually seeing a pink elephant. Similarly, people who talk about hearing themselves think or about listening to the voice of reason or conscience, or who say things like "I can still hear my mother saying 'Now, don't forget your galoshes,'" are not insisting that such experiences are exactly like or even especially similar to actually hearing someone speak. It is not clear exactly what such uses of 'see' or 'hear' are intended to convey. Presumably they indicate at least that the subject regards imagining an elephant as more similar to visually perceiving one than it is to other sorts of sensory experiences (e.g. smelling an elephant). Nevertheless, being more similar to visual perception than to other sensory experiences is compatible with otherwise little likeness between visually imagining and visual perception. (My uncle looks more like my aunt than he does my car, but he looks most unlike my aunt.) Perhaps such expressions are also attempts to characterize the experience in a way appropriate to its putative object—that is, perhaps I "hear" my mother's voice because auditory perception is the standard way of detecting voices.

In any case, an AHM conception of voices is not required merely by the fact that we customarily speak of hearing voices. One can speak of hearing voices without meaning to speak of auditory experience. The auditory hallucination explanation itself is rather that the experience of voices seems subjectively similar to the experience of actually hearing someone else speak, or is so much like that experience, that this explains the subject's strong or vivid impression that the voice comes from without—that it is another's voice. Presumably, hallucinators are as familiar as other people with the experience of listening to the voice of conscience, or hearing oneself think, or generally with what it is like to engage in inner speech. The idea is not that their having this sort of experience is supposed to explain the alien character of their verbal hallucinations. Rather, the idea is that, on some occasions, their experience of what is in fact their own inner speech *feels* or seems so much like their typical experience of hearing someone else speak that they have the powerful impression that they are hearing another speak.

Even if its truth is not guaranteed simply by the standard terminology for describing voices as things heard, the AHM provides us with a context for understanding what happens in verbal hallucinations.

To begin with the obvious, the AHM says that the study of voices should be a part of the general study of hallucinations. Hallucinations occur in all sensory modalities: visual, auditory, tactile, olfactory, and so on. So, one may expect an understanding of hallucinations in one modality to illuminate and to be illuminated by the study of hallucinations in other modalities. For example, Peter Slade and Richard Bentall criticize various accounts of verbal hallucinations—including Hoffman's (1986), which we discuss in the next chapter—on the ground that they do not generalize to other sorts of hallucinations. "Hoffman's account," Slade and Bentall write (1988, p. 134), "suffers from the problem that it seems only to explain auditory hallucinations. Hallucinations, however, may occur in other modalities."

Further, since hallucinations are generally thought to represent disorders or defects of perception, the broadest context in which to pursue an understanding of voices is that provided by the study of perception. "The implications of hallucinations for psychology," Slade and Bentall remark (ibid., p. 27), "are . . . considerable. As extreme forms of perceptual aberration, they present extreme tests for theories of perception."

Presumably the evolutionary job or adaptive function of sensory perception is to enable organisms endowed with it to identify features of or track changes in their environments (and sometimes also in their bodies). The process of tracking is complicated by the occasional need to discriminate perception-like experiences that are only in our heads from perceptions of extramental objects and events. Slade and Bentall refer to this as the problem of "reality discrimination" and maintain that hallucinations represent failures or breakdowns of reality discrimination: "Hallucinations result from a dramatic failure of the skill of reality discrimination, leading the hallucinating individual to repeatedly misattribute his or her self-generated private events to a source external to him- or herself." (ibid., p. 214) This leads Slade and Bentall to expect that hallucinations can be understood only if we understand the normal process or skill of reality discrimination, and that studying failures of this skill may help us to understand how it operates when it proceeds successfully:

To mistake the imaginary for the real presupposes that, ordinarily, it is possible to tell them apart. What is missing from existing accounts of hallucinations, then, is an explanation of how, under normal circumstances, most people can tell the difference between imagined events (i.e. experiences generated by themselves, occurring within their skin) and events in the external world. It is only by first understanding the mechanisms involved in this type of judgment that the circumstances under which these mechanisms fail will be understood. (ibid., pp. 205–208)

Thus, according to the auditory-hallucination model of voices, the implications of the study of verbal hallucinations for our understanding of human consciousness will be worked out in the context of a general account of perception and of perception's defects, and, in particular, with reference to the problem of reality discrimination.

3.4 Going in Circles

Before breaking off this rather general discussion of the AHM in favor of more detailed and specific examination of a particular version of the AHM, we need to address one more issue. We have mentioned that explanations of why a subject mistakes a hallucination for a perception in terms of alleged similarities between the experiences must be on guard against circularity. One must take care to avoid understanding similarity by reference to the subject's tendency to mistake one experience for the other.

Slade and Bentall (1988) are aware of this problem and take pains to avoid it. They make clear that according to them having a hallucination of a voice is not the same thing as believing that you really hear a voice. Many hallucinators, they note, know very well that their voices are hallucinations and that they are not actually hearing someone speak. "For this reason," they write, "it seems reasonable to require only that the experience (of hallucination) resemble in all respects the corresponding actual perception and not that the individual necessarily believes it to be real." (ibid., p. 24) Thus, the "similarity" between hallucination and corresponding perception is not a matter of the hallucination's being mistaken for perception.

Some authors use the expression "auditory" or "verbal hallucination" in a manner which entails that a subject who experiences verbal hallucinations *ipso facto* believes that the experience is "real" (i.e. perceptual). That is, verbal hallucinations, by such definition, involve delusional beliefs. In the AHM the relevant delusion would be the belief that one really is hearing someone else speak. However, as we will note again in discussing Hoffman's theory of voices, a great many subjects who experience voices do not have these convictions. In part, this is because it does not *seem* to them that they are having *auditory* experiences. However, even in such cases, there is another sort of delusion that might be said to be involved in verbal hallucinations. This is the belief that the "message" received when one hears the voice actually originates in or is sent by a nonself agency. We simply note here that our own use of the expression "verbal hallucination," like Slade and Bentall's, carries no implication that the subject has either of the beliefs mentioned above (or, indeed, any other delusional beliefs).

Slade and Bentall try to avoid the charge of circularity in their proposal to explain why hallucinations are sometimes mistaken for perceptions by reference to experiential similarities between the two types of experience. However, if this explanation is to have any definite content, it must specify the relevant similarities and demonstrate how they contribute to errors in reality discrimination. Here Slade and Bentall's analysis is not helpful. They claim that in hallucinations "the experience resembles in all respects the corresponding actual perception" (p. 24). However, it is clear that they do not mean *in all respects*. It is part of their account that hallucinations and corresponding actual perceptions have different etiologies (causal histories). Perceptions can be traced back to appropriate environmental stimuli; hallucinations are internally generated in the absence of such stimuli.

Commenting on Slade and Bentall 1988, Andrew Sims (1995) qualifies their claim concerning the resemblance between hallucinations and perceptions:

Subjectively, hallucination is similar to sense perception. (p. 78)

Subjectively . . . an hallucination is indistinguishable from a normal percept. (p. 83)

Sims's interpretation is a natural reading of what Slade and Bentall have in mind. However, for some philosophers and psychologists the appeal to "subjective" similarity raises suspicion and skepticism. It suggests an account of the similarity of experiences in terms of their "like-thisnesses," "phenomenal properties," "qualia," and the like. Partly because of worries associated with the metaphysical enigma of privacy (mentioned in chapter 2), some theorists doubt the cogency or intelligibility of such notions. Some question whether phenomenal properties can play any role in serious psychological explanations. It is not our intention to endorse or reject doubts about qualia. (At least one of us is unmoved by fear of qualia. See Graham 1998, pp. 8–14, 204–211, and 227–247.) We simply note that relevant similarities between experiences need not be a matter of shared phenomenal or qualitative properties. Recall the third condition in Slade and Bentall's characterization of hallucinations: that hallucinations are "not amenable to direct or voluntary control by the experiencer"

(1988, p. 23). Perhaps this is the relevant way in which they "resemble" their corresponding actual perceptions. Hallucination, just like perception, is not under voluntary control. In any case, whether explanation in terms of qualia or phenomenal properties is respectable or not, the AHM is not restricted to giving a phenomenal-property-based account of the similarity between hallucination and perception.

4

A First Tale of Hoffman

4.1 The Best of the AHM Accounts

What is the most fertile and best worked out AHM account of voices in the literature? Our vote goes to Ralph Hoffman's paper "Verbal hallucinations and language production processes in schizophrenia," published in *Behavioral and Brain Sciences* in 1986. Although we believe that Hoffman's account is inadequate and subject to serious objections, we believe that in many important respects it is on the right track. Even if it does not suffice as it stands, it offers elements of a more promising approach. Further, Hoffman's discussion assembles a wide range of evidence and explores connections between voices and a variety of issues in psychopathology and cognitive psychology. Reading the paper is a primer on the whole topic of verbal hallucination. Its value in this respect is enhanced by the many invited commentaries that accompany it (the paper is a *BBS* target article) and by Hoffman's replies. Finally, Hoffman is philosophically informed and is sensitive to questions which philosophers raise about voices.

In this chapter, we shall emphasize certain crucial differences between Hoffman's approach and alternative AHM conceptions.

The main topic of the first three sections of the chapter is what Hoffman's theory is not. In the rest of the chapter we explore what it is. The next chapter offers a constructive critique.

On page 504 of his 1986 paper,[1] Hoffman claims that verbal hallucinations are "instances of auditory imagery" (i.e., inner speech), and that the occurrence of such imagery is a "normal component of human consciousness." "This," he writes, "immediately raises the central issue of the paper. What specific features lead schizophrenic persons to experience certain instances of verbal imagery as if they were actually coming from another person?"

The bulk of Hoffman's paper attempts to provide a detailed and empirically well-supported explanation of the alien quality of voices—the fact that the voice seems to be that of another person. He offers what may be described as an honest-error or understandable-mistake account of verbal hallucinations. As Hoffman describes them, verbal hallucinations involve false beliefs on the part of the hallucinator, particularly the conviction that she is hearing someone else speak. However, although it is erroneous, Hoffman contends that this belief is reasonable for the subject in view of her subjective data or evidence. By this Hoffman does not mean that it is justified or warranted. He means merely that the belief has a rational basis sufficient to account for its acceptance by the subject.

Hoffman's explanation of the alien quality of voices entails that subjects take themselves to be hearing someone speak and that this mistaken impression plays a crucial role in explaining what makes the voices seem alien. This means that his account is a version of the auditory-hallucination model of voices. However,

---

1. All subsequent citations of Hoffman refer to this paper.

he gives the AHM a distinctive nonphenomenological twist. Most proponents of the AHM propose that there are phenomenological or "sensory" (Hoffman's term) similarities between voices and auditory perception and that these help to explain their alien quality. "How is it," asks Hoffman, "that many schizophrenics identify certain instances of verbal imagery as hallucinating? Most investigators have assumed that alterations in sensory features of imagery explain this." (p. 503) Hoffman takes a different approach. He complains that the sensory-quality approach "has not yielded a definitive picture of the nature of verbal hallucinations" (p. 503). He charges that appeal to phenomenological qualities of voices has proved unexplanatory, so he offers his own account as an alternative to it. His account appeals to similarities between voices and genuine auditory perception, but not to phenomenological or sensory similarities, as the best means by which to explain voices' alien quality.

4.2 A Touch of the Bizarre

To believe that one hears someone else speak, when no such speaker can be detected by other observers, has a touch of the bizarre. When these beliefs persist and get elaborated into imaginative stories involving communication with deceased or supernatural agents, implanted receivers, and so on, it is difficult to accept them as rational. Here two nonHoffmanian hypotheses about how people might come to believe such propositions suggest themselves.

(1) A subject's apparent failure to recognize that the voice is really her own inner speech is an instance of "motivated dissociation." Owing to unacceptable or undesirable contents of her own

thoughts, the subject is driven to disown them and to attribute them to another. "Often," Hoffman notes, "schizophrenic [voices] express ideas that are unacceptable or distasteful to the subject. This has led to a traditional psychoanalytical explanation of [voices] as expressions of wishes and motivations that need to be disavowed or disowned by the subject." (p. 515) On this motivated–dissociation account, the subject's conviction that the voice is that of another person rather than her own is a "dishonest" error: a piece of self-deception (since she can't be motivated to disown it unless, at some level, she first takes it to be her own).

If the motivated-dissociation story smacks of outdated Freudianism or self-help paperbacks, there is another nonmotivational way to explain the subject's error.

(2) Perhaps the subject has suffered some general cognitive breakdown that has rendered her incapable of reasonably evaluating the evidence or drawing rational conclusions from it. She suffers from thought disorder, is in the grip of schizophrenic logic, or is manifesting an underlying neuropathology. Though describing errors resulting from general cognitive breakdown as "dishonest" is clearly a strain, the breakdown account entails that there is no rational or evidential basis for the subject's error. It can be explained on the assumption that the subject (perhaps for reasons beyond her control) is unable to assess the truth of her belief by any rational strategy.

Of these two alternatives, Hoffman has more tolerance for the first, allowing that motivational elements may play a background or stage-setting role in explaining the alien quality of voices. Perhaps, for example, they help to bias a subject's estimation of the evidence for the origin of the voice. However, he denies that motivational factors are the whole or even a critical part of the tale (p. 515).

Hoffman allows that the second alternative "has some surface plausibility," but argues that research by Maher (1974) undermines attempts to trace the delusion found in schizophrenia back to "a primary disturbance in the logic of inferential processes" (p. 508). "It is hard," Hoffman writes, "to invoke such breakdowns in logic to account for [verbal hallucinations], for systematic study has demonstrated that schizophrenic subjects are no more prone to such inferential pathology than control groups." "Thus," Hoffman concludes, "the most plausible explanation is that the external misattribution of schizophrenic [verbal hallucinations] is a more or less justified inference derived from altered perceptual data." (ibid.)

Hoffman does not argue at length against either the motivational or the general-breakdown explanation of verbal hallucinations. Rather, he develops his own honest-error account. He tries to demonstrate that, in view of the success of the account, there is no reason to postulate cognitive pathology in order to explain the subject's belief in the alien character of her voices, and that motivational factors play, at most, a secondary, supporting role in such explanations. However, when it comes to the standard AHM line that subjects take certain of their episodes of verbal imagery to be alien because of special sensory or phenomenal properties, he offers a concerted counterargument.

The standard AHM line that Hoffman attacks can be described as follows: People's experience of their own inner speech normally has a very different "sensory feel" than, and is qualitatively quite distinct from, their typical experience of hearing someone else speak. Think of the qualitative difference between reciting Coleridge's "Kubla Khan" silently to yourself and hearing someone else read it aloud. The qualitative differences between the two sorts of experience provide at least part of the explanation of how subjects are able to distinguish them. If, for some reason, a subject's experience of his own inner speech has the same sensory feel as a typical experience of hearing another speak, then the subject may be expected to mistake such episodes of inner speech for auditory perception of another's speech. The alien quality of the voice would be accounted for by this qualitative similarity between the voice and typical instances of auditory perception.

Hoffman charges that the hypothesis that verbal hallucinations are qualitatively similar to typical instances of auditory speech perception lacks "solid empirical evidence" (p. 540). In spite of or perhaps because of the hypothesis's intuitive appeal, few attempts to test it have been reported in the literature. Mintz and Alpert (1972, p. 314) assert that imagery associated with voices is "more like external auditory stimuli in the dimension of vividness [than imagery associated with normal inner speech] and therefore [is] more readily confused with [imagery derived from external auditory perception]." However, this assertion represents an inference from their finding that hallucinating schizophrenics show a general tendency to experience all sorts of auditory imagery as particularly vivid when compared to controls. Hoffman cites other studies which have failed to find any such differences in the rating of auditory imagery (p. 504).

The results of the most direct test of the hypothesis that we have been able to locate were negative. John Junginger and Cynthia Frame (1986) asked patients to compare a "voice" actually heard through headphones with their most recent verbal hallucination. They found that "patients reliably report that a headphone 'voice' presented at levels approximating normal speech is louder, clearer, and more outside the head than their most recent VH" (Junginger 1986, p. 528). Junginger sums things up by suggesting that "it appears that hearing a hallucinated voice is not that different a sensory experience from normal verbal imagery, but it does differ from normal auditory perception" (ibid.). Hoffman (p. 504) endorses this conclusion: "How is it, then, that a VH can seem deviant or alien to the schizophrenic when no specific sensory features can be identified that contribute to this experience?"

Before explicating more of Hoffman's account, we shall discuss two proposals that he considers briefly. Neither identifies any specific sensory feature shared by voices and typical instances of auditory perception, though both advance interesting hypotheses that would account for why episodes of inner speech involved in voices might seem particularly vivid and external to their subject.

(1)   Slade (1976) and Hemsley (1982) suppose that hallucinators attend more intently to their inner speech than do normal subjects. Such enhanced inner attention may have the effect of making their inner-speech episodes appear more vivid or life-like than they seem to normal subjects.

Why should hallucinators, or at least those who suffer from schizophrenia, pay closer attention to their inner speech? Slade (1976) and Hemsley (1982) propose that schizophrenics tend to withdraw from external stimuli. Withdrawal may be due to sensory overload caused by problems with perceptual filtering or, perhaps, to their difficulty in making overall sense of external events.

Hoffman entertains an alternative explanation of enhanced attention in schizophrenia: Perhaps schizophrenics suffer from a general impoverishment of inner-speech production (p. 504). This means that whatever inner speech they do produce appears more striking to them.

Each of the above ideas—that of Slade and Hemsley and that of Hoffman—faces the same objection: It implies that, in vulnerable subjects, not just some but *all* of the subject's inner speech should seem particularly vivid and external. However, hallucinators do not generally experience inner speech as voices. Further, as Hoffman himself notes (p. 504), studies have failed to find any consistent differences between hallucinators and controls when they have been asked to rate the vividness of their voluntarily produced verbal imagery.

(2)   A proposal put forth by Christopher Frith in a 1979 article in the *British Journal of Psychiatry* titled "Consciousness, Information Processing, and Schizophrenia" draws its inspiration from what are known as "functional" hallucinations (Fish 1962). Functional hallucinations are based on perceptions of genuine external stimuli. For instance, Frith (1992, p. 68) cites a patient who reported "When the door slams I hear the words 'Get out.'" The notion is that verbal hallucinations represent mishearing or misinterpretation of genuine auditory events. The subject's attention is first drawn to some external stimulus, such as running water or a droning air conditioner. Frith supposes that the subject is primed or biased toward interpreting external auditory stimuli as the speech of another person. Given such a stimulus, the subject generates (in inner speech) interpretations of the stimulus as speech. Her awareness of these "interpretations" is what constitutes verbal hallucinations. Frith (1992) calls this the "input" theory of voices. On pages 68–71 of that book he abandons the input account he endorsed in his 1979 paper. Nevertheless, it is worth briefly

exploring the possibilities and problems associated with the input account.

4.3 The Input Account

The input account offers a ready explanation of the alien quality of voices. Voices sound external and other-produced to the subject because they are based on or incorporate genuine external stimuli. The subject is hearing sounds originating outside her, even if she is grossly "mishearing" or misinterpreting them. Thus, it is only to be expected that she should regard her voices as coming to her from without and as coming perhaps from another agent.

Further, the input theory may explain why voices are qualitatively similar to instances of auditory perception. In verbal hallucination the verbal message is supplied by the subject as a kind of shadow interpretation of the external stimulus, but the experience contains an element of genuine auditory perception. Voices are similar to auditory perceptions because they are, at least in part, auditory perceptions.

The idea behind input theory is not without some limited empirical support. Experimental work by Margo, Hemsley, and Slade (1981) and by Bentall and Slade (1985) indicates that schizophrenic patients known to suffer from verbal hallucinations are more likely than either nonhallucinating schizophrenics or normal subjects to misperceive nonspeech sounds as speech under a variety of conditions. Of course, such studies establish only that hallucinators are especially prone to interpret ambiguous or low-signal-to-noise-ratio auditory stimuli as speech, not that this is what is going on generally when they hear voices. However, they do at least fit with what would be expected if the input account of voices is correct.

But how does the input theory fare as a general theory of verbal hallucinations? Not well. As Hoffman observes, "a major limitation of the model is that it forces the conclusion that all hallucinatory experiences derive from external sound: this seems untenable, for schizophrenics are able to hallucinate quite actively in total silence" (p. 512). Patients in sensory-deprivation experiments sometimes experience verbal hallucinations (Slade and Bentall 1988, pp. 103–104; Frith 1992, p. 68). Contrary to the hopes of some investigators, the verbal hallucinations experienced in sensory deprivation turn out not to be closely parallel to the voices reported by schizophrenics. They tend to consist of isolated words rather than the more complex messages characteristic of schizophrenic voices. (Only 15 percent of such subjects report complex hallucinatory experiences. See Slade and Bentall 1988, p. 104.) Nevertheless, verbal hallucinations do occur under conditions where external auditory input is absent or minimal.

In response to evidence of voices in the absence of external input, Frith (1979) suggested that the input model might accommodate such cases by supposing that sensory-deprivation subjects mishear internal auditory stimuli, such as the sounds of their own heartbeat or respiration. This explanatory tactic, however, sacrifices the primary strength of the input approach. If sounds that provide the perceptual basis of voices come from within the subject's body rather than from the external environment, the input theory loses its ready explanation of the alien and specifically external quality of voices. Since the sounds originate within him, why does the subject have the impression that they come from without?

Even more damaging for input theories are reports of verbal hallucinations in deaf subjects (Slade and Bentall 1988, p. 30; Hamilton 1985). Critchley et al. (1981) provide a particularly interesting discussion of this phenomenon. Their subjects were diagnosed schizophrenics whose profound deafness either was congenital or occurred before the subject learned to speak. Ten of twelve patients reported experiencing voices. In one case, the patient was apparently having verbal *visual* hallucinations. He said that he could see someone address him in sign language. Others, however, insisted that they could hear the voices; that is, they used the sign for hearing to describe the experience even when questioned by the interviewer about their choice of words.

The empirical evidence discussed above is not intended to discredit the claim that some people experience functional verbal hallucinations (e.g., hearing "get out" in a door slam) or that hallucinators may show a distinctive tendency to mishear nonspeech sounds as speech. However, it does raise serious doubts about whether verbal hallucinators are, in general, functional hallucinations.

4.4   The Core of Hoffman's Account

We are now ready to take a first look at Hoffman's account of voices. This will reveal the core of his account and certain *prima facie* worries about it. We then will discuss how he develops his account to address those worries.

As we noted earlier, Hoffman, in common with most clinicians and other investigators, assumes that voices are self-generated verbal imagery or inner speech. He takes more than customary care to argue that inner speech occurs in connection with verbal hallucinations. He claims that awareness of self-generated verbal imagery constitutes the experiential basis for verbal hallucinations. From the perspective of this last claim, the striking or puzzling fact about voices is that, although the hallucinator is talking to himself, he believes that someone else is doing the talking and that he is only listening. That is, the subject misattributes the relevant speech or mislocates its source. The central problem, then, is to account for why the subject comes to mistake experience of his own inner speech for experience of someone else's speech.

Hoffman considers the possibility, mentioned above, that the explanation for the subject's error lies in special sensory or phenomenal features that distinguish voices from ordinary inner speech. However, he rejects this explanation, concluding that "the sensory properties of [voices] are not distinct from ordinary verbal imagery" (p. 503).

Hoffman proposes that another aspect of voices does properly distinguish voices from ordinary, self-attributed inner speech. He describes this aspect as their *apparent unintendedness*. According to Hoffman, the subject experiences voices as episodes whose occurrence is not intended by him. Voices appear to the subject as something that happens to him independent of (and, in many cases, even contrary to) his will or desire, and it impresses him that the speech is not under his control. In contrast, Hoffman implies, subjects ordinarily experience their own inner speech as under their control: as something they do or produce intentionally. According to Hoffman, then, voices are distinguished from ordinary experiences of inner speech in that voices are "verbal images that are experienced as unintended" (p. 505).

Voices are experienced as unintended, whereas ordinary inner speech is not. So says Hoffman. But how does this fact, if it is a fact, solve the problem of attribution to another agent? How does it explain the subject's impression that he experiences someone else's speech? Much more must and will be said, but the gist of Hoffman's answer is this: The explanation of the alien character of voices lies in the roles that both apparent intendedness and apparent unintendedness of verbal imagery play in our *normal* procedures for sorting out what we say to ourselves from what we hear other people say. Hoffman maintains that "a more or less automatic expectation or inference in normals is that unintended images are nonself derived" (p. 509). "This is plausible," he notes, "because the great abundance of images experienced as unintended during the day are sensory impressions derived from the outside world" (p. 509). They are unintended by us, at least.

Imagine that you find in your stream of consciousness both verbal images that constitute your own inner speech and verbal images derived from your auditory perception of other people's speech. To maintain your sense of the coherence of your own thinking and to follow what others are saying in your presence, you need a way to distinguish the images you produce from those that come to you from without. Hoffman claims that persons solve this problem, which we shall call the *fundamental attribution problem*, by noting whether a given bit of verbal imagery appears as intended or as unintended. Allowing for rare coincidences in which what we hear someone else say is exactly what we intend to say at the very same moment, verbal imagery that seems unintended to us typically is nonself derived; that is, the feeling of unintendedness is a reliable (albeit fallible) subjective indicator of nonself origin. Hence, I come to infer, more or less automatically, that if a given sequence of verbal imagery does not seem to me to be something that I intended to say, it is something that someone else said.

Supposing that we do use the above Hoffmanian strategy in solving the fundamental attribution problem, one should expect that, if an episode of my own inner speech seems unintended by me, then I would infer that it consists of perception of someone else's speech. That is, I will take unintended speech to be alien. So, if subjects experience voices as unintended verbal imagery, the above account explains why they also take them to be of nonself origin.

Hoffman's proposal for how we solve the fundamental attribution problem dovetails nicely with his supposition that a subject's misattribution of a voice can represent an epistemically honest error: a mistaken use of a normal sortation strategy. When a schizophrenic infers that his voices come to him from without, he employs the same procedure—the same method of solving the fundamental attribution problem—that normals use. He interprets felt or sensed unintendedness as a reliable indicator of alien origin. Further, this inference enjoys solid inductive support, since (according to Hoffman) "the great abundance" of apparently unintended verbal imagery is of alien origin. Unless the schizophrenic's impression that voices are unintended is somehow irrational or dishonest, his conviction concerning the alien character of a voice is reasonable on the basis of experiential evidence. We would all reach the same conclusion if we experienced what he experiences. No pathology or special motivation is required to make the inference.

4.5   First Critiques

Hoffman's core account of verbal hallucination seems to seriously overpredict the occurrence or the frequency of voices. Hoffman suggests that voices are relatively rare (which, if true, is fortunate, since he regards them as symptoms of a major psychiatric disorder). But unintended inner speech is a common phenomenon. We have all experienced lyrics of a song running through our heads, words or sentences coming unbidden into consciousness, and the spontaneous and seemingly undirected flow of interior soliloquy. If, as Hoffman's account proposes, apparently unintended inner speech is more or less automatically taken to be of nonself origin, all of the above would be experienced as alien—that is, would appear to us as voices. They manifestly do not appear so in most cases. We may sense that an episode of inner speech is unintended without ceasing to regard it as our own unintended inner speech.

But perhaps unintended inner speech is rarer than we suppose. Perhaps the examples mentioned above are not really cases of unintended inner speech. This raises two more difficulties with Hoffman's account: Exactly what does Hoffman have in mind when he describes verbal imagery as intended or unintended? What is it for subjects to sense or experience a bit of verbal imagery as intended or as unintended? To explore these two questions, we must turn to Hoffman's account of the information processing that subserves, or the psychological economy that underlies, the production of inner speech.

Hoffman supposes that inner speech, like overt speech, is "intelligent sequentially organized behavior" (p. 505). Citing work in cognitive psychology and artificial intelligence, he claims that our ability to engage in this behavior requires "the representation of plans that are precursors to the action itself" (p. 505). In the case of speech, he calls such precursor processes "discourse plans." Discourse plans specify high-level goals or objectives—to greet someone, to formulate a reply to an objection, and so forth. They also specify lower-level strategies for realizing these high-level goals. Suppose I want to defend my argument against an interlocutor's objection. I will need to adopt a particular strategy for this purpose—for example, accusing my opponent of begging the question. To execute this strategy, I must ultimately select and articulate some specific utterance, such as "But you are simply assuming what I deny in my first premise."

Hoffman acknowledges that cases in which we consciously are aware of even the high-level goals that direct a particular speech act are exceptions rather than the rule. However, discourse planning need not be at the forefront of conscious attention to be effective. Often the relevant high-level goals will be accessible on demand, or after prompting or encouragement, even if they are not in fact consciously accessed. However, it is plausible to suppose that low-level processes of discourse planning are never introspectively accessible, and that no prompt can unearth them and no session on a couch can elicit them.

Nevertheless, Hoffman proposes that his hypothesis about discourse planning "suggests an account of the experience of unintendedness that accompanies certain of our actions." "A nervous tic," he writes, "feels involuntary because it does not reflect a motor plan consonant with accessible goals/beliefs. Similarly, a slip of the tongue feels involuntary because it is not consonant with the current speech goal, that is, to articulate a particular message." (pp. 505–506)

Hoffman supposes that even when it does not occupy our conscious attention, discourse planning results in our having at least *tacit* expectations regarding what we are going to say—to ourselves or to others—on a particular occasion. These tacit expectations reveal themselves, e.g., in our unprompted recognition of verbal slips. I say, silently or overtly, "He struck him a blushing crow," and I realize immediately that this did not come out right. When our speech output fails to match our expectations, we experience the verbal imagery as unintended. In the normal case, where output is consonant with our expectations, we proceed happily or fluidly on our merry linguistic way.

Hoffman's notion of the intended is taxonomically nuanced. He distinguishes between "strong" and "weak" senses of 'intended'. Verbal imagery is strongly intended when it is "consciously decided upon" or "preceded by conscious decisions" (pp. 509–510). These are cases where a speaker explicitly considers or formulates at least the higher-level goals to be realized in a speech act. "Weakly intended" verbal imagery, by contrast, includes all cases in which the imagery produced is "consonant with consciously accessible" goals, whether or not the speaker actually accesses those goals. Presumably, any speech act that matches expectations will count as at least weakly intended. The expectation need not be explicitly formulated or considered.

The weakly/strongly intended distinction, though perhaps not terribly fine-grained, helps to answer the worry (mentioned above) about what Hoffman means by intended/unintended, and it permits Hoffman to make a preliminary response to the worry that his account overpredicts occurrences of verbal hallucinations. This concern is supported by the intuition that unintended inner speech is common whereas verbal hallucinations or voices are relatively rare. Hoffman can now try to explain away this intuition by arguing that it is based on the suggestion that inner speech is unintended unless it is strongly intended. This supposition makes it reasonable to claim that unintended inner speech is common, since relatively few instances of speech are strongly intended. Hoffman, however, can plausibly suggest that instances of inner speech normally are at least weakly intended. Thus, in the normal case, inner-speech output matches the *tacit* expectations derived from discourse planning and so is not experienced as unintended. Weakly intended inner speech does not trigger the experience of unintendedness and, hence, does not activate the nonself inference (i.e., does not get sorted into the alien category). Inner speech is missorted or misattributed only if it *fails* to match the subject's expectations. Such misattribution may be relatively rare.

4.6   Cognitive Breakdown and Schizophrenia

How does the subject of voices produce inner speech that fails to match his expectations? One way in which this could happen is if discourse planning were to malfunction. For example, suppose that there is disruption of the processes that take us from high-level goals to articulation of a particular message. I may want to say something to the effect that my opponent's objection begs the question, but, as a result of some malfunction in the planning process required to accomplish this purpose in a particular speech act, I wind up saying "My opponent denies what I deny." Hoffman contends that this is exactly what happens in schizophrenia. It is well known that many schizophrenics exhibit disordered overt speech. Hoffman quotes the following response from a schizophrenic patient to an interviewer's request "Tell me about school":

Well there are schools of play and schools of fish, mostly you see fish school, people edumacating [*sic*] themselves, you see, sea is one thing and education is another. Fish is school in their community, that's why the community of man stands in the way of the community of the sea, and once they see the light of sunny sunshine then they will let it be. (p. 507)

Citing a variety of studies, he claims that schizophrenic speech disorder reflects breakdowns in the planning processes that connect high-level communicative goals with specific speech output (pp. 506–507).

Hoffman proposes that disturbances of discourse planning also occur in the production of inner speech. These disturbances result in articulation of inner speech that fails to match expectations derived from higher-level goals and, hence, in inner-speech performances that are experienced as unintended by the subject. Following the standard fundamental attribution procedure, the subject will more or less automatically infer that the relevant verbal imagery is of external origin. That is, the subject will experience it as an alien voice. Presuming that such breakdowns in discourse planning are distinctively associated with schizophrenia (perhaps owing to the neuropathology of schizophrenia), this would explain the occurrence of verbal hallucinations in schizophrenia.

The above proposal raises a question: Why is *overt* speech not experienced by schizophrenics as nonself-generated? As Hoffman notes, schizophrenics do exhibit disorders of overt speech production. On his model, overt and covert speech production are both vulnerable to discourse-planning breakdowns, which in both cases result in mismatches between expectations and speech output. Shouldn't this lead the subject to experience his own overt speech as unintended (i.e., to experience verbal images derived from perception of his own overt speech as unintended)? If so, why doesn't this experience result in misattribution of the schizophrenic's unintended overt speech?

Hoffman has two replies to this. First, schizophrenics often do experience their own overt speech as unintended (Chapman 1966). However, in such cases, Hoffman writes (p. 510), "kinesthetic sensations that derive from motor aspects of speech production are strong immediate evidence that the speech is self-generated." This kinesthetic evidence blocks the nonself inference in the case of unintended but overtly articulated speech. This also explains why nervous tics and other involuntary bodily movements "are not subject to external misattribution" (p. 511).

Since the relevant sort of kinesthetic evidence is lacking in the case of inner-speech production, the nonself inference goes through. Second, "it also seems that at times the otherness inference can leak through during overt speech" (p. 510). Hoffman cites reports that schizophrenics sometimes experience their own overt voices as alien—i.e., attribute their own audible speech to another speaker (p. 504). Though such cases are less common than inner-speech-based verbal hallucinations, their occurrence would seem to support Hoffman's general approach, because his model offers a plausible explanation of misattributed overt speech. When overt speech fails to match expectations derived from discourse planning, it will be experienced as unintended; that is, verbal imagery derived from auditory perception of one's own overt speech will be experienced as unintended. This experience of unintendedness constitutes evidence that the relevant verbal imagery derives from perception of another's speech. Normally such evidence is overridden by kinesthetic evidence that the speech is self-generated, but one can suppose that occasionally kinesthetic evidence fails to block the nonself inference.

Although we do not want to examine the issue further here, it is worth asking how things seem to the Hoffmanian subject when he misattributes his own *overt* speech. Does he ignore the kinesthetic evidence and infer that he is not speaking (i.e. not opening his mouth, moving his tongue, and so on), or does he realize that he is engaged in such motor activities but feel that somehow these movements of his body, and the speech sounds they produce, are controlled by another and are being used to realize the other's speech intentions rather than his own? We shall discuss an issue intimately connected with this in chapter 6.

4.7   Inspecting Nonself Attribution

Hoffman's distinction between strongly and weakly intended inner speech helps him to respond to the worry that his model overpredicts the occurrence of voices. However, even if one grants that some purported examples of unintended inner speech are weakly intended, it is difficult to shake the conviction that unintended inner speech must be more common than voices: that people can and do experience episodes of inner speech as unintended without therein becoming convinced that the episodes are of nonself origin. Further, there is evidence (noted in chapter 2) that verbal hallucinations often occur in nonschizophrenic subjects. One must wonder, then, whether the association between schizophrenia and speech disorder provides much support for the hypothesis that there is a general association between verbal hallucination and discourse-planning breakdown.

Hoffman responds to these challenges by introducing two further distinctions. Parallel to his distinction between strongly and weakly *intended* inner speech, Hoffman distinguishes between strongly and weakly *unintended* inner speech. He also introduces a distinction between *true* verbal hallucinations (i.e., verbal hallucinations properly so called) and borderline or pseudo-verbal hallucinations. He deploys these distinctions in tandem: True verbal hallucinations occur only when inner speech is strongly unintended, but borderline or pseudo-hallucinations may occur when inner speech is only weakly unintended. This allows Hoffman to grant that not all episodes of unintended inner speech give rise to (true) voices, and they render the hypothesis that (true) voices are closely connected with schizophrenia more plausible.

Hoffman suggests that an inner-speech episode is *weakly unintended* just in case it fails to accord with cognitive goals of which the subject is or might become introspectively aware. Thus, an inner-speech episode counts as weakly unintended if it occurs in the absence of any accessible discourse goals or objectives. An episode is *strongly unintended* only if its occurrence conflicts with the subject's currently accessed cognitive goals. Thus, strongly unintended inner speech must occur in a context in which the subject takes himself to be actively pursuing some cognitive project other than the speech act in question. It is inappropriate to, and thus disrupts, his execution of that project.

A hypothetical example of strongly unintended inner speech serves to clarify the notion. Imagine a case of what we might call "Penfield speech"[2] : a subject's inner speech is caused by an electrode planted in the subject's brain (Penfield and Perot 1963; see also Wakefield and Dreyfus 1993, p. 260). Imagine that the speech seems grossly inappropriate to the subject relative to his current activity. (Suppose he is trying to solve a math problem, and the Penfield verbal imagery is of McGill University alumni slogans.) Penfield speech is not intended speech (on Hoffman's account), because it is not caused by discourse planning. And it would not impress the subject as his own imagery, because it is strongly unintended.

Hoffman holds that both weakly and strongly unintended inner speech are initially inferred to be of nonself origin. That is, both trigger (or are prone to trigger) nonself inference. Actually, Hoffman claims that the experience of unintendedness is "a nec-

2. In the 1950s, Wilder Penfield, a neurosurgeon at McGill University, mapped large regions of the cerebral cortex by applying electrodes to different areas in the brains of epilepsy patients. He found that stimulating certain points in the region elicited bodily motions, childhood memories, and fragments of long-forgotten tunes.

essary precursor to the generation of hallucinations" and seems to allow that it may be necessary but not sufficient for hallucinogenesis (pp. 508–509). However, when the relevant inner-speech episode is only weakly unintended, the initial nonself inference may be overridden or canceled by a sort of reality test (to be described later in this chapter). Hoffman describes such preliminary, labile impressions of nonself origin as borderline hallucinations or pseudo-hallucinations. In the case of strongly unintended inner speech, however, reality testing fails to cancel the nonself inference. Here the subject develops the persistent conviction or delusion that the relevant episode is of nonself origin. Hoffman reserves the term "verbal hallucination" or "true verbal hallucination" for such cases.

Is there experimental or clinical support for Hoffman's account of the experience of unintendedness? Hoffman, of course, claims that there is, and he cites several studies by David Foulkes and his collaborators (Foulkes and Fleisher 1975; Foulkes and Scott 1973; Foulkes and Vogel 1965) on an association between hallucinatory experiences and what Hoffman (p. 508) calls "passive consciousness."

Foulkes monitored normal subjects using electroencephalogram and electro-oculogram readings. At various points the experimenters would intervene (perhaps by awakening subjects) and ask subjects to report on the character of their mental activity just before the interruption. The experimenters distinguished four stages of consciousness, using EEG and EOG criteria. These ranged from relaxed nondrowsy consciousness (characteristic of daydreaming or aimless mentation), through drowsiness, to two levels of sleep. Hoffman describes the results as follows:

Clearcut hallucinatory experience, that is, imagery that is momentarily felt to originate from "outside" as opposed to being self-generated, was frequently reported for all four stages: 31 percent of mentation reports [for the first stage] contained hallucinations with progressive increases to 71 percent [for the final stage]. Because the hallucinatory character of these experiences during wakefulness was only fleeting, Foulkes [and collaborators] termed these experiences "borderline" hallucinations. (p. 508)

Hoffman draws two conclusions from Foulkes's data. The first is that they "clearly indicate that the nonself attribute can be assigned to images during normal waking states of consciousness" (p. 508). That is, normal subjects are prone to regard certain instances of self-generated imagery as alien, at least "momentarily," under some (not particularly unusual) conditions. Second, on the basis of his own review of the data in Foulkes and Vogel (1965), Hoffman observes that

the data [indicate] increases in the frequency of mentation that the subjects experienced as involuntary in passing from relaxed wakefulness to [final stage] sleep. These increases from stage to stage closely paralleled and were somewhat greater than—the observed increase in the frequency of frank hallucinosis (i.e. momentarily believing that the image was from the "outside"). The stage-to-stage statistical dominance of involuntary images compared to frankly nonself experienced images suggests that the former is a preliminary condition for the introduction of the latter during normal cognitive states. (p. 509)

In short, borderline hallucinations—i.e., momentarily accepted nonself inferences—arise from imagery that the subject experiences as unintended.

Hoffman takes the experimental findings described above to support his proposal that all subjects more or less automatically infer that apparently unintended verbal imagery is of nonself origin (p. 509). However, since such inferences are only momentarily accepted by normal subjects, it seems that there must be some process that normally cancels or undoes such inferences.

Clinical studies by G. Sedman (1966a) may suggest something about the nature of this canceling process. Sedman describes pseudo-hallucinations as images that were experienced as if they were perceptions from the outside but where the impression is recognized as untrue. He uses the expression "true hallucinations" to designate experiences having exactly the same perceptual attributes as "pseudo-hallucinations" except that the patient had a sustained conviction that the perception had a nonself origin. Sedman studied groups of patients, one composed of nonpsychotics and affective psychotics, the other of schizophrenics. He found that 50 percent of patients in the first group reported pseudo-hallucinations but that no nonpsychotics and only one of the 14 affective psychotics reported true hallucinations. Among the schizophrenic group, however, 12 of 16 patients reported true hallucinations; only 3 reported pseudo-hallucinations. Interestingly, Sedman found that schizophrenics reported a dropoff in the frequency of hallucinations as they passed from "clear" to "drowsy" consciousness—"exactly the opposite of the trend reported by Foulkes and his colleagues for 'borderline hallucinations' of normals" (Hoffman, p. 509).

Taken together, Hoffman suggests, the studies by Sedman and those by Foulkes and his collaborators indicate that borderline or pseudo-hallucinations are common among nonschizophrenics, and that true hallucinations tend to be associated with schizophrenia. Both classes of hallucinations share the same introspective attributes and both involve at least momentary commitment to the nonself inference. What distinguishes true hallucinations is that in the true case the subject sustains his commitment to that inference, whereas in the pseudo case it is somehow undone. This suggests that the schizophrenic has true hallucinations, because the reality-testing process that corrects mistaken nonself inference in others fails to work in his case.

What is the nature of the reality test? Hoffman proposes that in nonschizophrenics the occurrence of unintended inner speech is typically associated with "passive cognitive states" (daydreaming, drowsiness, and so on). He hypothesizes that in such states there is an "absence of concordance between cognitive goals" and speech output, because there is an "absence of *any* cognitive goals during passive cognitive states" (p. 509). Failure of concordance causes inner-speech output to be experienced as unintended, and this triggers the nonself inference. However, some process normally undoes these mistaken inferences. "This self-corrective process," Hoffman writes (p. 509), "reflects the normal emergence from a passive to an active (i.e. goal-directed) cognitive state; one can presumably learn that unintended or alien representations occur during prior passive states and thereby dismiss their veracity." That is, subjects discover that there is an association between making mistaken nonself inferences and being in passive cognitive states. This leads them to discount such inferences on reflection, when they return to an active state of consciousness. Hoffman adds this (p. 509): "We frequently do not simply discount our daydreams as unreal, but rather momentarily enter into them as if they were objectively real only to disclaim them later when the salience of the outer world is increased."

However, suppose that one were to produce unintended speech while engaged in active, goal-directed mentation. The reality test proposed above would be powerless to correct a mistaken nonself inference made while one is in an active cognitive state. "The felt nonconcordance between verbal imagery and cognitive goals," writes Hoffman (p. 509), "would reinforce the alien sense of the image and sustain external misattribution." This, Hoffman argues, is precisely what happens in schizophrenia. The schizophrenic's discourse-planning processes are not idling or offline when he hears voices; they are malfunctioning. Hence, the schizophrenic tends to produce unintended inner speech when he is actively pursuing or attempting to pursue some (other) goal-directed cognitive task. As nonschizophrenics do, the schizophrenic more or less automatically infers that the relevant verbal imagery is of nonself origin. But when he applies the standard reality-testing procedure to his inference, the test confirms the nonself inference, since the unintended imagery occurs in active rather than passive consciousness. The subject sustains his commitment to the mistaken inference and thus suffers a true verbal hallucination.

Hoffman notes (p. 509) that this account neatly explains Sedman's "paradoxical observation that drowsy states of consciousness practically eliminate true hallucinations among schizophrenic subjects." Mistaken nonself inferences made while the subject is drowsy will be detected and overridden by the standard reality test. Thus, the subject will not report that he really heard voices while he was drowsy.

Hoffman also notes (p. 509) that his account supports the contention that "the nonself inferences that underlie [voices] are in themselves nonpathological." On his view, they represent honest epistemic errors based on subjectively available evidence, and the inference from the experience of unintended verbal imagery to the hypothesis that the imagery is of nonself origin is "plausible because the great abundance of unintended images experienced during the day are sensory impressions that actually derive from the outside world" (p. 509). Similarly, the reality-testing strategy employed by the schizophrenic is normally reliable. Since most people's discourse-planning processes are in good working order, most people produce unintended inner speech only under conditions in which those processes are not engaged—i.e., conditions of passive consciousness. The schizophrenic falls into persistent delusions that most of the rest of us escape, not because we are better inductivists or better able to face the truth about ourselves, but because his peculiar pathology defeats the very same reality resting that saves us from such delusions.

More generally, Hoffman's account of verbal hallucinations locates them against the background of normal cognitive functioning and speech sortation. We are all faced with the fundamental attribution problem: the need to distinguish inner speech from verbal imagery associated with perception of other people's speech. We solve this problem by means of the same two-stage strategy that schizophrenics use. This consists of a preliminary screening stage where we take felt or sensed unintendedness as the mark of external (nonself) origin, and then a backup reality-testing process that catches misattributions of inner speech made in the first stage. If cognitive functioning is normal, this backup process will catch nearly all misattributions. Verbal hallucinations (true verbal hallucinations) occur when low-level cognitive malfunctions (discourse-planning breakdowns) cause the subject to produce unintended inner speech that sneaks past the backup process. Roughly, discourse-planning breakdown causes the subject to produce unintended inner speech in circumstances in which the backup process is not looking for it. We need not suppose that hallucinators are distinctively irrational: that they make inferences via "schizophrenic logic," or have suffered some general cognitive breakdown. Nor need we search for motivational factors: special anxieties or emotional needs to disown or to escape responsibility for thoughts and impulses. The hallucinator's pathology does not impugn his cognitive or emotional normality. Rather, it forces him to confront a situation in which normal cognitive processes lead him astray.

Is Hoffman's theory of nonself attribution in voices on the right track? Where, if at all, does it go astray?

5

A Second Tale of Hoffman

5.1 The Akins-Dennett Regress Objection

Theories take risks. No theory carries a guarantee of success. Hoffman's theory of the nonself attribution of voices seems vulnerable at various points, strong at others.

Central to Hoffman's account of voices and their alien character is the hypothesis that inner-speech acts are intended or unintended and somehow are experienced or appear as such. In one of the many commentaries on Hoffman's paper that appeared along with his target article, the philosophers Kathleen Akins and Daniel Dennett charge that the notion of intended or unintended inner speech creates a problem for Hoffman's account. Here is how they state the problem:

Hoffman's account is threatened by (inter alia) an infinite regress: If we identify "slips of the tongue" as misexecutions of . . . intentions, relative to what could there be "slips of thought"? Wittgenstein thought that "slips of thought" were impossible because a mistake presupposes an intention. Although we can intend to reach a particular (cognitive) conclusion—say, discovering a new way to drive home from the office—we cannot intend each of the thoughts that constitute our attempted derivation or discovery, on pain of generating a never-beginning regress of intentions to form thoughts. Some thoughts must just "come to mind," however apt, well-ordered, and useful they prove to be in the larger project. (Akins and Dennett 1986, p. 517)

Akins and Dennett do not make the regress threat to Hoffman's account entirely clear. The reference to Wittgenstein's (1982) view—that slips of thought are impossible because a mistake presupposes an intention—seems to indicate that they see a regress looming behind the notion of having an intention to think or to form a thought. Their subsequent discussion, however, suggests that this notion of intending to form a thought is problematic or regressive only if it is carried too far— that is, only if it is taken to mean that each and every thought is intended.

Is there some absurdity in the very notion of intending to think? If we assume that an overt action counts as intended (or as a "slip") in virtue of its relation to the agent's previous thoughts, then, presumably, a thought is intended (or is a "slip") also relative to the agent's previous thoughts. Obviously, this account of the intendedness of thoughts combined with the thesis that each and every thought is intended leads to a "never-beginning" regress. However, nowhere does Hoffman imply that every thought must be intended.

It is also true that the question of intendedness seems not to arise for some things called "thoughts." Consider, for example, the type of thoughts which philosophers classify as propositional attitudes (Graham 1998, pp. 5–6; Heil 1998, pp. 132–133). It is at least a bit odd to describe someone as intending to *believe that p*, or *hope that q*, or *intend that r*. One may have a desire to *believe that p* and intend to induce this belief: one notable way in which to do that is to focus attention on certain kinds of evidence for "p". But intending to induce is not intending to believe. In the case of propositional attitudes themselves, it seems that one just has them, responding to the moment-to-moment forces (in the case of belief, to perceptual evidence or argument) acting upon one. However, Hoffman's account explicitly concerns only inner speech: the sort of verbal imagery that he supposes is involved in voices. The assertion that one intends to say something to oneself is no odder than the assertion that one intends to say something aloud (perhaps to another). Just as one may mis-execute an intention to talk aloud, one may mis-execute an inner-speech-act intention.

Suppose I intend to recite, silently, the last line of "Kubla Khan," but I say to myself "For he on doney hew hast fed and drunk the milk of paradise." That would count as a mis-execution of an inner-speech-act intention.

Admittedly, as we noted in chapter 2, inner speech serves as a paradigm or a stereotype for thinking generally. Thus, when we imagine someone thinking, we often depict the individual engaging in inner speech. If one conceives of *believing that p* as a matter of saying to oneself "p", then one's suspicions about the idea of intending to think, or intending to believe, spill over onto the notion of inner-speech intentions.

Though surely there is some sort of association between propositional attitudes (e.g., beliefs) and inner speech, it is a mistake to regard believing as a matter of saying something to oneself, or even as a matter of being disposed to say something to oneself. In part, this is a mistake for the same reason it is a mistake to regard propositional attitudes as dispositions to overt speech. On the one hand, one may have propositional attitudes which one is not disposed to express to others or to oneself. On the other hand, one may say to oneself "p" without believing or even understanding what one says. One may say to oneself "In

Xanadu did Kubla Khan a stately pleasure dome decree" without believing or even comprehending what one says. Meanwhile, efforts to analyze believing as saying to oneself sincerely,
assertively, and with semantic comprehension are likely to end in
explanatory circularity, presupposing the very notion of believing
that one hopes to capture by the analysis. What, for example, is
saying something sincerely to oneself other than saying it while
believing it?

It seems a mistake to depict cognitive mental activity generally—"thinking" in its broadest or most general sense (including propositional attitudes)—as inner speech. Talking to oneself is
a way of thinking, but it seems a relatively sophisticated and special
way of thinking. I talk to myself in English. We conduct our inner
speech in conventional human language. Indeed, there is evidence
that the ability to engage in inner speech depends on first learn-
ing to speak aloud (Hoffman 1986, p. 505). It seems doubtful that
all cognitive activity, even all human cognitive activity, employs
conventional languages. Our brains may use mentalese or perhaps
a variety of so-called languages of thought, but we do not talk to
ourselves in mentalese. We talk to ourselves in the same languages
we use when we talk to others.

In supposing that inner speech is intended or unintended,
then, Hoffman does not commit himself to the thesis that propositional attitudes or cognitive activities generally are perspicuously
described as intended. Nor does the hypothesis that inner speech
may be intended lead to a regress. One may ask: "If a subject per-
forms an inner-speech act intentionally, he must have had the
intention to perform that speech act. What then of the intention?
Did the subject also intend to form the intention to perform the
speech act?" However, the answer to these questions is irrelevant
to whether the subject's speech act was intentional. Intentions are

the sorts of mental states that call forth or direct actions. An action, inner or outer, is intentional just in case it is properly brought about by an intention. However, whether the intention itself is formed intentionally has nothing to do with whether the act that stems from it is intentional. There is thus no reason to regard intended inner speech as the unattainable end of an infinitely regressive series of intentional acts.

Hoffman does subscribe to a thesis that looks more vulnerable to a charge of regress, however, and this may be the thesis that Akins and Dennett wish to attack. In defending the postulation of discourse planning behind speech, Hoffman writes (1986, p. 505):

Workers in cognitive science and artificial intelligence have convincingly argued that even modest attempts to model intelligent, sequential behavior require the representation of plans that are precursors to the action itself.

The implied argument, which may be called the Planning Argument (PA), goes something like this:

PA1:   Intelligent, sequential behavior requires planning.

PA2:   Inner speech is intelligent, sequential behavior.

PA3:   So, inner speech requires planning.

PA produces a regress problem. The regress problem generated by PA is that discourse planning would seem to be intelligent, sequential behavior. Hence, from PA1 it seems to follow that

PA4:   Discourse planning requires planning, viz., discourse-planning planning.

Meanwhile, discourse-planning planning is just as intelligent and sequential as discourse planning, so it will require further planning, and so on.

Since Dennett delights in exposing explanations of intelligent behavior that presuppose the intelligence they seek to explain, it is a good bet that this is the regress he and Akins have in mind. At some point one must (we assume) cease explaining intelligent performance by intelligent planning; otherwise intentional-level explanation will have no end and offer no theoretical enlightenment.

What should Hoffman do in response to the Akins-Dennett regress argument so understood? If Hoffman somehow restricts PA1 so that discourse planning itself does not require intelligent planning, he faces the following dilemma: If discourse planning can be explained without presupposing that it is planned, then why not inner speech itself? Of course, advocates of intentional or cognitive psychological explanation make their theoretical livings by arguing that, just because intelligence at *some* point must be explained without assuming intelligence, that does not mean that intelligent action at *every* point must be explained without assuming intelligence. One of the most popular strategies in cognitive science consists of analyzing the activities of a cognitive or intelligent system into component functions, themselves operating intelligently, and then to seek nonintentional mechanical explanations for the most basic and barely cognitive components (Bechtel, Abrahamsen, and Graham, 1988). William Lycan (1987, p. 40) describes this strategy of cognitive scientific research as follows:

We explain the successful activity of one homunculus [i.e., intelligent system] . . . by positing a *team* consisting of several smaller, individually less talented and more specialized homunculi—and detailing the ways in which team members cooperate in order to produce their joint or corporate output.

More to the present point, however, Hoffman's basic account of nonself attribution in voices does not require anything as strong as PA1. His model requires only that inner speech is intended or unintended. This requirement may be plausible independent of his discourse planning story of just what it means for inner speech to be intended or unintended. One could defend the point that inner speech is intended or unintended without endorsing the Hoffmanian tale of discourse planning.

Unfortunately, however, there is another regress problem with Hoffman's model. This one seems to have escaped notice by Akins and Dennett. And it is serious, for it is associated with Hoffman's account of self-attribution.

5.2   Another Regress Objection

Consider an inner-speech act, T, which the subject self-attributes (from the outset). On Hoffman's basic model, the subject self-attributes T because T accords with the subject's inner-speech-act intention, IT. We argued above that whether IT is intended is not relevant to whether the subject intends T. However, it may be very relevant to whether the subject self-attributes T. Suppose that IT is not intended; then, by a very natural extension of the basic Hoffmanian model, the subject will not self-attribute IT. However, if he does not regard IT as his own intention, it would be very strange were he to attribute T to himself on the basis of its concordance with IT. Presumably the subject would take the concordance between T and IT as a ground for self-attributing T only if he thought of IT as his own. Recall that the Hoffmanian subject of voices supposes that his voices accord with *somebody's* intentions; he just doesn't believe that the voices accord with his own intentions.

Hoffman seems to face a dilemma. On the one hand, he can agree that the relation between T and IT offers grounds for self-attributing T only if IT is self-attributed, and that IT is self-attributed only if it is intended. In this case, sticking with his model, he will have to postulate a further intention, IIT, in order to explain the intendedness and self-attributedness of IT. However, IIT itself will have to be intended and self-attributed in order to account for the self-attribution of IT. And we're off on a regress: IT, IIT, IIIT, and so on. On the other hand, Hoffman can allow that the concordance of T and IT provides grounds for self-attributing T only if IT is self-attributed, but attempt to account for the subject's self-attribution of IT without supposing that IT is intended. Or, perhaps, he can try to explain the intendedness of IT without postulating any further intention with which IT accords. In either case, self-attribution of IT will work differently than self-attribution of T. The fundamental attribution problem will be solved differently in the two cases. However, this invites the following objection: If the self-attribution of IT can be explained without postulating intentions to intend, why not explain the self-attribution of T without postulating inner-speech-act intentions? The objector may conclude either that Hoffman's account of self-attribution leads to an infinite regress or that it is explanatorily otiose.

We believe that Hoffman can avoid this objection. However, there is a tax to be levied.

First, there is the issue of avoidance. The foregoing dilemma assumes that concordance between inner-speech act and inner-speech-act intention accounts for the subject's self-attribution of the act only if the subject also self-attributes the inner-speech-act intention. Hoffman rejects this assumption. On the basic model, the facts that the subject has the intention IT and that his inner-speech act T actually accords with IT are jointly sufficient for the subject's initial self-attribution of T. He need not believe that he has the intention. Perhaps, should the subject believe that he has no such intention, IT, he would reconsider his self-attribution of T. However, the self-attribution of intention plays no role in Hoffman's model. Indeed, it will be recalled, he assumes that we have no conscious access to or awareness of our discourse planning (at least in its multi-level totality). Something in us responds to or attends to the concordance or the failure of concordance between inner-speech acts and inner-speech-act intentions. This "something in us" determines whether a given passage of inner speech strikes us as intended or as unintended. Our sense of intendedness provides the proximate basis for self-attribution or nonself attribution. But Hoffman insists upon no conscious, personal-level comparisons of acts against their underlying intentions.

Hoffman may thus avoid the dilemma posed by the objection. But now comes the tax.

The main question of how self-attribution works for intentions (and propositional attitudes and thoughts generally) does not go away. We do ascribe intentions and other propositional attitudes to ourselves. It just doesn't seem plausible to claim that such self-attributions depend on the presence of subconscious or subpersonal intentions to intend to intend or to believe. So, even if Hoffman's model accounts for the self-attribution of inner-speech acts, it leaves the self-attribution of other mental activities a mystery. It fails to generalize to those activities.

We need some account of psychological self-attribution in addition to the sort of account of inner speech that Hoffman offers. Moreover, if we need this additional account anyway, then why not use it to explain self-attribution of inner speech? The suspicion that Hoffman's account may be unnecessary—the suspicion that nonself attribution of voices may be accounted for in different and non-intentional terms—is a problem for this account, even if we assume (as we do not further debate here) that threats of infinite regress finally have been or can be removed.

5.3   Self-Attribution, Introspection, and Attitudes

To defend Hoffman's account of voices, one must explain what it is about inner speech that makes it plausible to think that self-attribution of inner speech works differently than self-attribution of thinking generally, including, most specifically, propositional attitudes (e.g., belief and intention). It would also be helpful to have an explanation of how self-attribution of inner speech fits into the general project of psychological self-attribution.

First, why think that self-attribution of inner speech works differently than self-attribution of, say, propositional attitudes? The following answer seems plausible.

No fundamental attribution problem arises for propositional attitudes, except possibly in special cases (such as the alleged phenomenon of co-consciousness in multiple personality disorder, which we will discuss in chapter 6). Other people's attitudes do not appear to me in my stream of consciousness; I don't seem to myself to have your beliefs or hopes occurring in me. Thus, we have no need to sort out our own beliefs or hopes from those of others. However, the attributional situation regarding inner speech is quite different. Although we do not perceive other people's inner speech, verbal representations derived from their overt speech appear in our consciousness along with verbal representations which constitute our own inner speech (and, of course, representations derived from our own overt speech). We therefore have to keep track of which verbal representations originate in us and which derive from others. Since there is no comparable attribution problem for propositional attitudes, it would be surprising if self-attribution did not work differently in the two cases.

Then how does self-attribution work for propositional attitudes? The following answer seems plausible if controversial.

Not only do we not perceive other people's beliefs and intentions, we do not perceive our own either. Propositional attitudes do not appear in or present themselves immediately or directly to own consciousness; they are not introspectible. Instead, they are a kind of theoretical-functional entity useful (indeed, perhaps essential—see Graham and Horgan 1994) for prediction and explanation of behavior. We infer their existence in ourselves in much the same way that we infer their existence in others (Graham 1998, pp. 42–86).[1] We attribute intentions, say, to other persons based on, roughly, their behavior and on our general background common-sense understanding and psychological theories of human behavior. I ascribe to Sam the desire to build a dome because he says things like "I will build a dome," because he engages in nonverbal behavior that seems directed at dome

---

1. This point—that we infer attitudes in ourselves in much the same manner as we infer attitudes in others—is aptly captured in an anecdote about the actress Marilyn Monroe. There have been several dozen biographies of her. To their readers, she may by now seem transparent in her attitudes. However, her sense of her own attitudes was a source of confusion and incomprehension to her. "I seem to have a whole superstructure with no foundation," she once mentioned to reporters, "but I'm working on the foundation." (Ludwig 1997, p. 13) She observed how she behaved and what others said about her, and she made inferences about her attitudes—inferences of whose fallibility she was despairingly convinced.

building, and because I accept a theory or understanding of Sam that links such overt behavior to his internal states (desires and intentions). In particular cases, theory may play a dominant role. Suppose, for example, that I believe Sam to have incestuous desires, although I have never observed him engaging in incest-directed behavior. Say that I attribute Oedipal desire to Sam because, for better or worse, I accept a Freudian theory of human psychology according to which everyone has that desire.

The above account of how we come to attribute particular propositional attitudes to ourselves denies that we have intro-spective access to our attitudes. Some philosophers will regard this as a defect in our account. They would maintain that not all of our (correct) self-ascriptions of intentions or beliefs can be explained as inferences based on theory or our observation of our own behavior. So, they conclude, we must have introspective access to at least some of our attitudes.

If "behavior" here is restricted to overt behavior (bodily movement), then the notion that we self-attribute attitudes not purely based on observation of our own behavior is sound. However, the conclusion that we *introspect* or are directly acquainted with our own attitudes does not follow.

Self-attribution of attitudes is often based on observation of our own inner speech (our saying this or that to ourselves). That is, just as we generally suppose that others have the intentions which are normally expressed by their overt speech acts, so we suppose that we ourselves have the intentions normally expressed by our own inner-speech acts. Likewise, just as in the case of infer-ences to others' intentions, inferences from inner speech to our own intentions are fallible and corrigible and may be blocked by contextual factors. If, for example, in the course of reciting

Coleridge's poem I say to myself "I would build that dome in the air," I do not attribute to myself any dome-building intentions. The context is poem recitation, not engineering. Moreover, inference from inner speech is not our sole access to our intentions and attitudes. There is access from overt behavior and theory. There is also access from the bodily sensations and emotional feelings often associated with and therein symptomatic of attitudes. I feel hungry, and feeling hungry is often associated with the desire to eat. It is not essential to the desire. The desire can be present without the feeling. The feeling, as victims of certain physical illnesses know, can also be present without the desire. However, the occurrence of the feeling can reliably signal the presence of the desire and elicit the self-report "I desire to eat."

That we often rely on introspective awareness of inner speech and feelings in discovering our own attitudes may explain the intuition that we have direct introspective access to propositional attitudes themselves. What is sensible in that intuition is the idea that introspective access of *something* plays a role in our coming to know what we desire or what we believe. We do not acquire such knowledge simply by observing our overt behavior or applying general theories to our own case. Introspection makes a significant contribution to our knowledge of our own attitudes. But it need not make this contribution by directly revealing our propositional attitudes to us.

A final misgiving about our claim that one's attitudes aren't introspectible: It may be charged that our account of propositional-attitude attribution combines with Hoffman's model of inner-speech attribution to form a vicious circle. I attribute intentions to myself on the basis of inferences from my inner speech. Meanwhile, I attribute inner-speech acts to myself on the basis of their concordance with my intentions. However, there is no circularity here, because different intentions are involved.

The intentions relevant to self-attribution of inner-speech acts are intentions to perform inner-speech acts. The intentions I ascribe to myself by inference from my inner speech are generally not speech-act intentions. For instance, if I say to myself "I will build a dome," I will normally ascribe to myself the intention to build a dome, not the intention to say to myself "I will build a dome." Should I say to myself "I will say to myself, 'I will build a dome,'" the intention I would ordinarily ascribe to myself is the intention to say (silently) "I will build a dome." To the extent that we ever attribute inner-speech-act intentions to ourselves, we may rely heavily on psychological theories (such as Hoffman's theory of discourse planning). As we noted in section 5.2, self-attribution of such intentions plays no role in Hoffman's basic model of inner-speech attribution. Thus, the intentions relevant to the self-ascription of inner speech are not the same as ones we naturally ascribe to ourselves by inference from our inner speech. Hence, it is not the case that one and the same intention both is self-ascribed by inference from inner-speech acts and serves as the basis for self-ascription of those speech acts. If it were one and the same intention, then there would be an explanatory circle—but since it's not, there isn't.

There is good reason, then, to suppose that self-attribution works differently for inner speech than for propositional attitudes. Further, Hoffman's account of inner-speech attribution fits naturally into a more complex account of self-attribution of psychological states and activities. We attribute various propositional attitudes to ourselves in part because we suppose that they are the attitudes expressed in our inner speech.

5.4 Discourse Planning, Inner Speech, and the Experience of Unintendedness

What exactly is the role of discourse planning in Hoffman's account of voices?

According to Hoffman, what happens when a subject suffers a verbal hallucination occurs in four steps:

(i) The subject produces verbal imagery or inner speech.

(ii) The subject experiences this inner-speech episode as unintended (by him).

(iii) This experience of unintendedness induces him to infer ("more or less automatically") that the relevant verbal imagery is of nonself origin (comes from another person).

(iv) This conclusion is submitted to reality testing, where it may be "undone" or canceled, in which case the subject's initial experience of alienation counts as a borderline or pseudohallucination. If reality testing fails to undo the initial impression that the verbal imagery is alien, then the subject is said to have undergone a "true" verbal hallucination, or a voice properly so called.

Discourse planning figures in the first, the second, and the fourth of these steps.

In the first step, Hoffman (1986, p. 565) holds that we must assume that discourse planning occurs in order to account for the subject's ability to produce intelligent, sequentially ordered inner speech.

In the second step, failure of inner-speech output to accord with goals or expectations incorporated in the subject's discourse planning explains why he experiences a given inner-speech episode as unintended. Failure of concordance may occur in two ways. In some cases, the subject may produce inner speech in the absence of any goals or expectations regarding inner-speech output. This is what happens when the subject produces inner speech while in a state of "passive consciousness":

The absence of cognitive goals can produce unintended images. This is reasonable given that the absence of concordance between cognitive goals and cognitive outputs such as action and speech predicts the experience of unintendedness. In the absence of *any* cognitive goals during passive cognitive states . . . no goal concordance is possible and imagery production will be experienced as unintended. (ibid., 509)

However, where discourse-planning processes are malfunctioning rather than absent, the subject may produce inner speech that clashes or conflicts with his current cognitive goals. Here inner-speech output is not merely unexpected; it is contrary to what the subject expects to say to himself. In this case, as in the first, the subject will experience his inner-speech output as unintended.

When the subject experiences an inner-speech episode as unintended, in either of the scenarios sketched above, he infers that the episode is alien. However, the specific causal history of his experience of unintendedness determines whether the resulting nonself attribution will be undone—in the fourth step—by reality testing. Reality testing is sensitive to whether the subject's impression that a given instance of verbal imagery is alien arose when the subject was in a passive cognitive state. Nonself inferences made in passive consciousness are discounted; otherwise the inference is sustained.

Thus, whether an experience of unintended inner speech is due merely to the absence of current cognitive goals or to a conflict between output and current cognitive goals ultimately determines whether the subject suffers a pseudo-hallucination or a true verbal hallucination or voice.

Assumptions about discourse planning put meat on the bones of Hoffman's basic model of voices. They give descriptive content to his notion of unintended speech and to connections between this notion and other elements in his model of nonself attribution. However, they also invite serious questions about whether this account is consistent and whether it can do justice to the data on verbal hallucinations.

There seems to be a conflict between Hoffman's assumption that discourse planning is required for the production of intelligent, sequentially organized speech and his assumption that the subject sometimes produces inner speech in the absence of discourse planning (i.e., when in passive consciousness). One way to remove the appearance of conflict is to insist that inner speech produced in passive consciousness is not intelligent or sequentially organized. But this move is implausible. Hoffman lists "daydreaming" and "free association" as activities that typically occur when the subject is in states of passive consciousness. However, the inner speech involved in such states is often extensive and coherently organized, even if it is not appropriate in the context of the subject's realistic longer-term goals. For example, if I slip into a athletic fantasy while trying to finish grading papers from my logic class, the daydream itself is likely to involve sequentially organized inner speech.

Whatever may be the case regarding daydreams, Hoffman cites evidence that the inner-speech episodes involved in verbal hallucinations (true or borderline) tend not to be "very creative or expressive and frequently consist of a small number of rigidly repeated expressions" (1986, p. 514). He speculates that they may involve "parasitic" memory representations "triggered by widely dissimilar and distant associations" (pp. 513–514). Presumably these representations are not current discourse plans. Perhaps

Hoffman can account for production of inner speech in the absence of discourse planning in this way.

However, the above considerations raise a more general and less avoidable issue. Hoffman supposes that whenever unintended inner speech occurs in the context of either passive or active consciousness, it is unplanned (i.e., not specified by relevant discourse goals). This suggests that such inner speech should be unintelligent: disorganized, random, lacking salience for the subject (Rund 1986). However, as numerous investigators have noted, voices seem both intelligible and intelligently directed to the subject, though it does not seem to the subject that he is intelligently directing them. Voices often are experienced as addressed specifically to the subject. They are appropriately structured to serve communicative goals, including warning, commanding, criticizing, consoling, and advising. Moreover, the subject generally regards their content as salient to his current character or situation. Doesn't all this suggest the presence of some sort of discourse planning—by Hoffman's own criteria—on the subject's part, though perhaps planning to which he enjoys no conscious access?

Some comments by Hoffman (1986, pp. 514–515, 530) indicate that he may be prepared to explain the apparent intelligence of voices as a product of the subject's attempt to "make sense" of the voice, ex post facto, rather than as a result of planning. That is, since the subject takes the voice to originate in another speaker, he will presume that it expresses the other's intentions and will supply or confabulate an interpretation that makes sense of those intentions. So perhaps the voice need not be really intelligent, in which case it need not be the product of discourse planning.

Whether or not the apparent intentionality of voices can be explained as the product of ex post facto interpretation, the "intelligence" of voices raises questions about Hoffman's contention that the subject's misattribution of a voice is an honest error. He pictures misattribution as the result of the application of standard or normal sorting procedures to abnormal data of a type which he takes to be unique to schizophrenia. The subject simply follows the same sortation or fundamental attribution procedure we all follow for distinguishing self-generated from other-generated verbal imagery. He gets the wrong result because malfunctioning discourse-planning processes (associated with schizophrenia) cause him to produce unintended verbal imagery in the context of active consciousness. It's a mistake we would all make in the same circumstances or condition. However, this story explains only why the subject mistakenly takes an inner-speech episode to be a perception of someone else's speech. It does not explain why he takes the voice to be addressing him, or talking about him. Nor does it explain why hallucinators so often regard the message expressed by the voice as salient to their situation and their concerns. These are further conclusions (i.e., they go beyond mere external misattribution), and, unless they are also honest errors, they provide an opening for those who would explain verbal hallucinations as products of irrationality or motivated self-deception and without recourse to discourse plans.

5.5   Silent Radios

As we have seen, Hoffman supposes that human beings have a system or procedure for distinguishing what they say to themselves from what they hear others say to them—that is, for distinguishing self-generated imagery from imagery that enters consciousness via auditory perception of another's speech. Verbal hallucinations stem from a breakdown in that system.

Self-generated verbal imagery gets mistaken for or misclassified as auditory perception of another's speech. We noted that Hoffman rejects efforts to explain such errors of attribution by appeal to sensory or phenomenal similarities between voices and genuine instances of auditory perception. Instead, he explains why the subject takes himself to be hearing another speak in terms of what may be called the "action-like" attributes of voices. The relevant similarity between episodes of verbal imagery experienced as voices and those resulting from a subject's perception of another's speech is that in both cases the imagery is experienced as unintended and is so experienced just when the subject is in a state of "active" consciousness.

In this section, we shall object less to Hoffman's specific account of how the subject comes to mistake her inner speech for a perception of someone else's speech, than to the supposition that hallucinators mistake inner speech for auditory perception. We shall argue that, in many cases standardly classified as verbal hallucinations, subjects do not take themselves to be *hearing* anything, nor do they have the impression that they hear someone (anyone) speak. We maintain that voices are not, in general, *auditory* hallucinations. In addition, we shall show that, even when subjects correctly recognize the nonperceptual, internal character of a voice, it may retain its alien quality. Thus, the hypothesis that subjects mistake voices for perceptual experience does not provide a general explanation of the alien quality of voices.

Our criticism of Hoffman in this section dovetails with the misgivings about the Kinsbourne whisper hypothesis, which we discussed in chapter 2. The whisper hypothesis proposes that the subject's auditory perception of his subvocal speech provides the experiential basis for his verbal hallucinations. But if voices are often not experienced as things *heard*, that raises questions about whether they need have any basis in auditory perception. More important, our criticism of the thesis that subjects mistake voices for perceptual experiences tells not only against Hoffman's account but against any version of the Auditory-Hallucination Model.

In her book *What I Saw at the Revolution*, former presidential speechwriter Peggy Noonan recounts the following incident from her days in Washington (1990, p. 121):

In the park across from the White House there was a man who handed out leaflets. "Are you being mind controlled by the subliminal radio? The government has developed a vast secret department involved in the study and advancement of mind control of individuals and groups by silent radio. As a dog hears a silent whistle, these persons hear the silent radio, which sounds the same as thoughts in their mind."

Though this is hardly the point of Noonan's anecdote, her story directs our attention to a serious problem for the Auditory-Hallucination Model of voices.

The AHM supposes that the experience of verbal hallucination is like the experience of hearing someone else talk to you. However, clinicians and patients alike have often noted that the experience of "hearing" voices need not be auditory or audition-like. For example, Eugen Bleuler, one of the great figures in the history of the study of schizophrenia, noted that for many patients "the voices are unlike spoken voices but are as of thoughts" (1934, p. 50). In his classic analysis of schizophrenia, *Dementia Praecox or the Group of Schizophrenics*, Bleuler remarked that patients often characterize their voices as "soundless" and as like "vivid thoughts" (1950, p. 110). He quotes a patient report of a command hallucination:

It was as if someone pointed his finger at me and said, "Go drown yourself." It was as if we were speaking to each other. I don't hear it in my ears. I have a feeling in my breast. (ibid., p. 111)

G. Sedman's careful study of patient experiences of verbal hallucinations provides several relevant examples. One patient said of her voice "I felt it within me. It doesn't sound as though it's outside." (Sedman 1966b, p. 487) Other patients described their voices as "within my mind," "in my head," and as appearing like "a loud, strong thought" (ibid., pp. 487–488).

These reports bear out a long tradition in clinical lore, dating back to Baillarger (1846) and Maudsley (1886), in which verbal hallucinations are understood as "interior voices, thoughts . . . rather than words actually heard as through the ears" (Flor-Henry 1986, p. 523). Baillarger noted that for many patients the voice seems to come not from without but from "the interior of the soul." He introduced the terms "psychosensory" and "psychic hallucinations" to distinguish verbal auditory hallucinations from nonauditory experiences (ibid., p. 523).

Recent discussions in the clinical literature continue to remark on the nonsensory character of some voices. John Cutting (1995, p. 17) observes that "some patients do not completely distinguish (voices) from their own thoughts." M. E. Garralda (1984), reporting on verbal hallucinations in children, observes that they did not generally seem to come from without but were "most often located in inner space." Laura Miller (1996) reported that, of the 50 subjects in her study of verbal hallucinations in post-treatment schizophrenias, 28 said that they experienced continued verbal hallucinations and knew of the hallucinatory nature of the experience. Although 10 of Miller's subjects described their voices as "indistinguishable" from auditory perception, 17, who claimed to have "vivid" voice experiences, said that they were "clearly distinct from real perception."

In the most direct study of whether voices are audition-like, Junginger and Frame (1985) asked 26 hallucinating patients to rate their voices according to whether they seemed either "inside the head" (i.e., similar to the typical experience of one's own inner speech or verbal imagery), or "outside the head" (i.e., similar to the typical experience of hearing another speak). Junginger and Frame offered the patients a 1-to-10 scale, with 1 indicating something clearly inside the head and 10 clearly external. They found that 11 of their subjects (41 percent) rated their voices at 5 or below, whereas 15 (59 percent) rated them from 6 to 10. A substantial minority of their subjects reported that "hearing" voices is more like "hearing yourself think" than it is like hearing somebody talk.

A possible complicating factor in the Junginger-Frame study is the extent to which the subjects' beliefs about the reality of their voices or their beliefs about their doctors' preferred view of their voices may have influenced patient reports. Many hallucinators, even many schizophrenic hallucinators, know that nobody is really talking to them. Nearly all also realize that their doctors disbelieve that anybody is talking to them. These facts alone may lead them to describe their voices as "soundless" or "like thoughts," even if their experiences are robustly audition-like. If the voice is really only in my head, or if I believe that my physician wishes me to admit that the voice is only in my head, I may be tempted to describe it, contrary to phenomenology, as thought-like. Or one may suppose, as does Hoffman, that the phenomenology of voice is cognitively penetrated or shaped by a subject's intellectual convictions about the reality of the voice.

Perhaps once I admit that the voice cannot really be alien, I cease to experience it as auditory.

However, there is solid evidence against any such attempts to explain away reports of nonauditory voices. First, Bleuler (1950, p. 110) notes that even when patients recognize that they are not *hearing* the voice, they may continue to regard it as "real" (that is, as truly alien, or as somehow attributable to another agent):

Many patients do differentiate between what they really hear and what is "imposed" on them. Nonetheless, even they are frequently inclined to attribute reality to the "voice."

Bleuler's point is well illustrated by this vivid case description (Allen, Halpern, and Friend 1985, p. 603):

The voices are not received as auditory events coming from without through the ears. . . . They feel distant and diffuse, "like thoughts," she adds ironically. "Ironically" because she cannot accept them as her own thoughts, but as messages sent to her by a being external to herself.

Chapman and Chapman (1988, p. 175) describe patients in their study as follows:

Many of our subjects describe vivid *inner voices* . . . Yet there is a striking variation in beliefs about these voices. The most common interpretation was that their voice represented their own conscience. . . . A few subjects, however, believed that the voices represented the intercession of other people. . . . A few subjects had *outer voices*. Again some subjects recognized these voices as products of their own minds, while others developed delusional beliefs concerning their origins.

Finally, when Junginger and Frame (1985) asked their subjects to report whether they regarded their voices as "real" or as "only imaginary," they found that subjects who rated their voices as "inside the head" were no less likely to rate them as real than were those who rated the experience of the voice as very similar to auditory perception. Conversely, subjects who said the voice definitely seemed to come from outside the head were just as likely to regard the voice as imaginary as subjects who did not experience the voice as auditory.

What is the theoretical lesson here? It is that many people who experience voices are not having auditory hallucinations. They do not mistake their awareness of inner speech for auditory perception of somebody else's speech, nor do they even have the impression that they are hearing another speak. Thus, verbal hallucinations cannot be regarded, in general, as an audition-like experiences. Furthermore, even when a subject recognizes that she is not hearing anyone else speak, she may continue to regard the voice as alien: to attribute it, somehow, to another agent or person. All this shows that neither Hoffman's account nor any other version of the AHM can provide an adequate general explanation of the alien quality of verbal hallucinations. According to every version of the AHM, the subject's having the impression that she hears her voices plays an essential role in her inference that the voices are alien. What the clinical findings recounted above reveal is that, in many cases, subjects take the voice to be alien even though it does not seem to them that they heard the voice. Thus, we need some other account of the alien quality of voices—an account that explains how voices can be experienced as alien without being experienced as auditory.

Let us be clear about what we are *not* claiming here. We do not deny that there are verbal auditory hallucinations. In his 1989 book on deafness, Oliver Sacks offers a particularly striking account of verbal auditory hallucination. First, Sacks quotes a passage from David Wright's (1969) narrative of his own experience of deafness[2]:

[My deafness] was made difficult to perceive because from the very first my eyes had unconsciously begun to translate motion into sound. My mother spent most of the day beside me and I understood every word she said. Why not? Without knowing it I had been reading her mouth all my life. When she spoke I seemed to hear her voice. It was an illusion. My father, my cousin, everyone I had known retained phantasmal voices. That they were imaginary, the projections of habit and memory, did not come home to me until I had left the hospital. One day I was walking with my cousin and he, in a moment of inspiration, covered his mouth with his hand as he spoke. Silence! Once and for all I understood that when I could not see I could not hear. (Wright, quoted in Sacks 1989, pp. 5–6)

Sacks then remarks:

This hearing (that is, imagining) of "phantasmal voices" when lips are read is quite characteristic of the post-linguistically deaf for whom speech (and "inner speech") has been an auditory experience. (p. 6)

We also are not saying that verbal auditory hallucinations should be distinguished from voices. The very evidence that we cite to show that some voices are not auditory (Junginger and Frame 1985) reveals that some voices are auditory. More exactly, it shows that some patients report audition-like or sensory elements in their experience of voices. This raises a thus-far-unmentioned theoretical possibility. Even if the AHM cannot provide an explanation of the alien quality of all voices, perhaps it can offer an explanation of those voices that are audition-like. Maybe it can explain the alien quality of verbal *auditory* halluci-

2. Wright became deaf well after he had learned to speak; thus, he had grown accustomed to listening to others speak.

nations properly so called. Frith (1992), for example, recognizes that some verbal hallucinations are not audition-like, but he offers an AHM explanation for why those that are audition-like appear alien. However, we would like the reader to entertain, at least, an alternative proposal for how to explain the alien character of audition-like voices.

Hoffman allows that voices are similar in their "sensory" qualities to instances of auditory perception. However, he denies that their alien character can be accounted for in terms of those sensory qualities. Being audition-like is not part of why they are experienced as external and alien. Rather, Hoffman's account runs the other way. Subjects first judge that they are hearing another speak on the basis of the apparent unintendedness of the experience, or its un-action-like elements; then this judgment alters (cognitively produces) the phenomenology (Hoffman 1986, pp. 504 and 515). The alteration causes subjects to regard "hearing" the voice and genuine auditory speech perception as similar experiences. If Hoffman's idea is on the right track, it might work as he says for the auditory character of audition-like voices. Audition-likeness would be an effect rather than a cause of alienation. To illustrate: A subject first comes to the conclusion that she is receiving a communication from another person or agent. The communication is alien. This, in certain cases, leads her to suppose that she must be hearing someone talk, which, in turn, makes it seem to her that she is hearing something. She seems to hear a voice.

There is interpretation here, but not in Dennett's ontologically confabulatory sense (discussed at the end of chapter 2). In his view there are, strictly speaking, no such things as phenomenal experiences, audition-like voices, or other subjective qualities in experience. However, the phenomenological idiom is practically unavoidable, and we should see what we can do to make sense of it in what Dennett calls their "heterophenomenological" interpretation.

However, Hoffman, as we just noted, is not claiming that nothing possesses phenomenal qualities. Quite the contrary, he says that there are voices (verbal auditory hallucinations), and that they are or can be audition-like. The element of interpretation that Hoffman advocates depends on the cognitive penetrability of auditory experience. He allows that subjects have a 'sensory' experience of their voices, but denies that this explains the alien character of voices. According to him, the nonself inference determines the phenomenology of voices, rather than vice versa.

Our suggestion—that is, Hoffman's suggestion—cannot be properly integrated into an overall account of the alien quality of voices until we offer an alternative account of the experience of alienation within one's own stream of consciousness, and, in particular, until we consider a second disorder common in schizophrenia (namely, delusions of thought insertion). However, we would like the reader to keep the suggestion in mind. Call voices "voices"; recognize that some (but not all) are audition-like; but, then, look for the explanation of their alien quality outside of their sensory or phenomenal qualities.

5.6   Reality Testing

We are getting somewhat ahead of ourselves. Before we leave this chapter on Hoffman, let us see if there are other elements in his account of voices that may be useful in constructing our final account.

As we noted in chapter 4, Hoffman invokes reality testing as the mechanism that undoes, or in unfavorable circumstances fails to undo, experiences of an alien sort (voices). Is this notion of reality testing worth preserving?

Certainly the idea is too simple as Hoffman describes it. He proposes that a subject notes whether an experience of alienation or nonself inference occurred in the context of passive consciousness and cancels the "passive" inferences while letting the rest stand. However, this seems to entail that passive nonself inferences get canceled even if their conclusions are true. That is, if the subject, while in a state of passive consciousness, perceives another person's overt speech and infers (correctly) that his experience is of nonself origin, he will cancel this nonself inference once he realizes that it occurred in the context of passive consciousness. However, presumably people do frequently (and correctly) come to believe that they heard another's voice while in a state of passive consciousness. If Hoffman's story is correct as it stands, people will regard all their "passive" speech perceptions as pseudo-hallucinations. Quite obviously and fortunately this does not happen.

A more plausible version of the reality-testing hypothesis is that, rather than automatically canceling nonself inferences made during passive consciousness, reality testing merely induces the subject to withhold judgment on or reconsider such nonself inferences. There are, after all, a variety of sorts of evidence to which one might appeal in trying to decide whether one "heard" one's own inner speech or actually heard someone else speak. In the latter case, a relevant speaker or device for transmitting speech must have been present, for example. Further, overt speech can be heard by persons other than the subject and could be recorded, so why not suppose that the subject can make use of these additional sorts of evidence in deciding whether a given episode of verbal imagery was of internal or external origin?

This raises a question about Hoffman's honest-error explanation of *delusions* of auditory alienation (i.e. true verbal hallucinations). Even when the subject "hears" a voice in the context of
active consciousness, there usually is abundant evidence that the
voice was internal. Hallucinators may well take some account of
this evidence, since they often confabulate rather remarkable and
very implausible stories to explain their voices—for example, that
the voice comes from God, or a demon, or a deceased relative, or
that it is transmitted to them via special "receivers" (silent radios)
hidden in their bodies. Such stories seem to be designed to
explain why the voice is not audible to bystanders, or why its
speaker cannot be found in the relevant vicinity. The hallucinator's
failure to make use of evidence of internality and his proclivity
to offer fantastic explanations of negative evidence tempts one to
say that his problems involve more than having experiences of
unintendedness while in active consciousness, and that they may
involve some deeper irrationality or powerful motivation to
alienate in his delusions.

The main evidence for Hoffman's reality-testing hypothesis
comes from studies (Foulkes and Vogel 1965; Foulkes and Scott
1973; Foulkes and Fleisher 1975; Sedman 1996a) which establish
that nonpsychotics have experiences of alienation and, hence, that
such experiences are not sufficient for delusions of alienation
("true" hallucinations). Hoffman believes that these studies show
that the presence of passive consciousness has a protective or pro-
phylactic effect for schizophrenics with respect to delusions of
alienation. Schizophrenics, like normals, tend to have experiences
of alienation (pseudo-hallucinations) while in passive consciousness. However, reality testing discounts such experiences in schizophrenics just as it does in nonpsychotics. That is, schizophrenics
don't have true hallucinations in passive consciousness, because

they recognize their suspicious nature via reality testing. Such "passive" experiences of alienation turn out to be mere pseudo-hallucinations. However, contrary to Hoffman, Sedman's data actually show, not that schizophrenics correctly recognize passive experiences of alienation as pseudo-hallucinations, but that they seldom report pseudo-hallucinations. Fifty percent of Sedman's nonschizophrenic subjects reported pseudo-hallucinations, versus 3 of the 16 schizophrenic subjects.

Though the small sample should discourage ambitious generalization, Sedman's study does not support the hypothesis that reality testing keyed to passive consciousness accounts for the protective effect of passive consciousness in schizophrenics. It's not that subjects discount passive experiences of alienation; they simply don't seem to be having passive experiences. Hoffman's reality-testing story may still remain a possible explanation of why nonschizophrenics don't go on to develop delusions despite their proclivity for experiences of alienation. If schizophrenics possess a distinctive tendency to have experiences of alienation while in active states, the reality-testing story may explain why they develop delusions of alienation. However, Sedman's data do not provide the sort of link between these findings that Hoffman needs.

Then how does the subject arrive at the conclusion that the voice is alien if not by reality testing? Hoffman offers no explanation of why the experience of unintendedness leads to the nonself inference unless it is by the route just sketched.

It is also worth noting that Foulkes and Vogel (1965) have shown that not all experiences of unintendedness imagery trigger the nonself inference. Hoffman (1986, p. 509) remarks that their report "indicates increases in the frequency of mentation that the subject experiences as involuntary in passing from relaxed wakefulness to [the second stage] of sleep," and that "these increases from stage to stage closely parallel—and were somewhat greater than—the observed increases in the frequency of frank hallucinosis (i.e. momentarily believing that the image was from the 'outside')." In other words, there are instances in which subjects experience their inner speech as unintended but do not take it to be of nonself origin. Thus, the nonself inference is a less automatic response to the experience of unintendedness than Hoffman elsewhere suggests.

The findings of Foulkes and Vogel are consistent with the hypothesis that inner speech can be experienced as unintended without being misattributed to another speaker, even momentarily. Commenting on Hoffman's paper, Junginger (1986, p. 528) offers another example:

Obsessional patients, for example, report a variety of thoughts, images, and impulses that are clearly perceived as unintended but not as nonself. Assuming that these patients experience these intrusive cognitive events during active consciousness, how is it that psychosis does not "quickly ensue"?

Other investigators have noted this feature of obsessional thinking. Fish (1985, p. 43) comments that "while the obsessed patient recognizes that he is compelled to think about things against his will, he does not regard the thoughts as being foreign, i.e., he recognizes that they are his own thoughts." If Fish is right, obsessional thoughts are experienced as unintended ("against his will") but not as alien.

Since Hoffman does seem to concede the possibility that inner speech is sometimes experienced as unintended but not misattributed, he might make a similar concession regarding obsessional thoughts. He might say that obsessional thoughts are experienced as unintended but not for this reason misattributed. In this case, however, he refuses the concession. In response to Junginger, Hoffman (1986, p. 536) denies that obsessional thoughts are experienced as unintended, in his understanding of that concept:

Although it is true that obsessional thoughts cannot be controlled, obsessive thoughts . . . are not unintended in the sense in which I have defined the term. Obsessives generally have ready conscious access to the goal of their obsessive-compulsiveness. . . . Though the obsessive is dominated by one or more maladaptive goals, his . . . thoughts are quite concordant with them. The prediction is that . . . obsessives who become psychotic are the ones who cannot access the goals that organize their behavior and therefore fear being controlled by outside forces.

Hoffman's point appears to be this: Obsessive thinking is intelligent (it is "thinking") in some sense; it is intended and experienced as such. As an obsessive hands washer, I may wash and re-wash my hands. The washing and re-washing is intended in the sense that is it undertaken to achieve some goal (clean hands, anxiety reduction, whatever). Even though I may wish that I could refrain from washing, I appreciate, at some level, that I wash intentionally albeit obsessively. (We shall return to the topic of obsessive-compulsive thought and behavior in our final chapter.)

Further comments in Junginger's discussion of Hoffman raise an interesting issue that bears on the question of what explains the alien quality of voices:

Obsessions are not typically perceived as voices of course, which raises a question not addressed by [Hoffman's] model. That is, without reference to the frequency of verbal imagery during normal cognition, the frequency with which some schizophrenics hallucinate seems to suggest that verbal imagery is a more prominent part of their thinking. The alternative is that [voices] are unrelated or only partly related to the occurrence of verbal imagery. The question of whether it is the patient's verbal imagery or his thoughts . . . that become "audible" is important. If verbal imagery is not integral to the perception of [voices], then phenomena such as obsessions and thought insertion are not distinguishable from [voices] on the proposed model. (ibid., p. 528)

As we will examine later, there is a strong potential affinity between voices and experiences of thought insertion. Both involve alienation or misattribution to an other. Hoffman also associates voices and thought insertion (which he calls "thought control"), noting that both are "strongly unintended experiences" that involve "internal representations nonconcordant with current epistemic goals" (p. 510). Junginger apparently supposes that Hoffman would distinguish voices from inserted thoughts on the ground that the former involve verbal imagery whereas the latter do not.

Truth be told, it is not obvious how Junginger himself distinguishes verbal imagery from thoughts, although he clearly thinks that there is a distinction, since he regards "the question of whether it is the patient's verbal imagery or his thoughts" that form the basis of voices as theoretically important. In any case, in view of Hoffman's insistence that "verbal images are a normal component of human consciousness whose frequent occurrence during cognition has been extensively investigated," together with his suggestion that "no specific sensory factors" or "primary sensory factors" distinguish verbal hallucinations from the normal verbal imagery associated with cognition, it seems doubtful that Hoffman would deny that thought insertion involves awareness of verbal imagery (p. 504). If Hoffman does regard verbal hallucination and thought insertion as distinct phenomena, he probably would claim that in the former case the verbal imagery seems "audible" (i.e., it seems to the subject as if she *hears* the voice), whereas in the latter case she does not suppose that she is hearing anything. Junginger may have the very same claim in mind; however, it is not clear how he would distinguish thoughts and verbal imagery.

All of this raises two questions.

Hoffman supposes that both verbal hallucinations and experiences of thought insertion involve nonself inference. Thus, on his view, a subject does not need to suppose that an episode of verbal imagery enters her consciousness specifically via auditory perception in order to regard the imagery as alien. Hence the first question: What accounts for the alien character of inserted thoughts?

Junginger suggests, and we have noted, that subjects of voices often believe that they are not *hearing* voices even though they suppose that they are experiencing the voice of another person. Hence the second question: Is there any special distinction between voices or verbal hallucinations and inserted thoughts? If not (and here is a promising theoretical possibility, on our view), perhaps a single general explanation can account for them. A univocal tale may explain the alien quality of voices as well as delusions of thought insertion.

Let us now sum up what we have done with Hoffman and anticipate where we will go from here.

Hoffman, as we have seen, explains the alienation or nonself attribution of voices by reference to the apparent unintendedness of relevant inner-speech episodes or verbal imagery. In this and the preceding chapter, we defended this strategy against objections to the very idea that inner speech or comparable mental activity can be intended or unintended. We defended the idea because we like the idea. Or, to be more exact, we like the idea (central to Hoffman's account) that people possess a sense of themselves as agents in at least some episodes in their mental lives. I may have a sense that *I* said this, or that *I* thought that. I may also have a sense that *I* did not say this, or that *I* did not think that, despite my recognition of the subjectivity (the presence within my stream of consciousness) of the relevant verbal imagery.

We shall call this impression that we are actively involved in certain episodes in our mental lives the sense of *mental agency*. Hoffman makes the sense of mental agency central to his account of voices. Such centrality—regardless of Hoffman's specific description of it in terms of discourse planning in the case of voices, reality checks, and the like—impresses us as an extremely helpful contribution to the explanation of the alien quality of voices, and perhaps also to the explanation of delusions of thought insertion.

But if the sense of mental agency is important in understanding voices (and delusions of thought insertion), what about Hoffman's portrayal of that sense and its role in the nonself attribution of voices? His portrayal is beset with difficulties. We have discovered at least four:

• We have learned that it is not plausible that every apparently unintended inner-speech episode is "automatically" taken to be of external origin, even subject to later correction.
• We have learned that appealing to discourse planning to explain unintendedness is problematic and perhaps dispensable.
• We have learned that the distinction between true verbal hallucinations and pseudo-hallucinations, although perhaps helpful for understanding active and passive consciousness in schizophrenia, is not useful for understanding voices.
• We have recognized that something can count as a voice without being experienced as audition-like or mistaken for sensory perception of

another's speech. Voices can seem alien even when they do not seem to be external.

Thus, we need to go beyond Hoffman. We need to examine thought insertion and its potential explanatory connection with voices. We need to school ourselves in the sense of mental agency that may figure in nonself attribution. We also need to propose an alternative account of the connection between unintendedness and alienation. This alternative account should not rely on invoking discourse plans or reality checking mechanisms. It should provide the self-conscious subject with the option of regarding apparently unintended thoughts as merely unintended but still the subject's own.

6

Thought Insertion

6.1 Just What the Theorist Ordered

Although some version of the auditory-hallucination model may explain the alien quality of some voices, it fails to provide a generally adequate account. Where should we turn for an account that covers the "nonsensory" voices that elude the AHM's grasp? To explore this question, we will examine another (or what is commonly considered to be another) sort of experience of alienation. This experience, mentioned in the preceding chapter, is *thought insertion.*

Prima facie, thought insertion is just what the theorist ordered. As with voices, the object of alienation, so to speak, is an episode of inner speech or verbal imagery—i.e., a thought. However, here there is no issue of the subject's confusing the thought with an auditory perception, since the subject explicitly describes it as a thought. Thus, chances seem good that whatever explains the alien character of inserted thoughts may likewise capture the alien quality of "nonsensory" voices. Indeed, it may capture the alien quality of *all* voices if the Hoffmanian thesis of cognitively generated phenomenology mentioned in the preceding chapter is correct.

Because the very idea of thought insertion seems odd, we need to consider whether "thought insertion" involves an unusual, distinctive form of self-experience rather than a metaphorical description of something more familiar, or perhaps mere verbal incoherence. We must take care in presenting thought insertion's clinical credentials. Once we have scrutinized the clinical phenomenon, we will consider various attempts to explain the alien character of inserted thoughts. This consideration provides the context in which we develop our own account of alienation.

As we mentioned in the first chapter, our account requires that we distinguish between two senses in which an episode of conscious mental activity may be "mine or "not mine." In order to motivate the distinction and make it clear, we shall begin by introducing the ultimately false or misleading hope that the study of thought insertion can contribute to resolving a long-standing debate about the metaphysical nature of self-consciousness (Stephens and Graham 1994). Explaining why this hope is forlorn will enable us to locate more precisely the difference between the two senses in which a mental activity can be said to be "mine" or "not mine."

The disturbance or misattribution in thought insertion is sometimes described as an internal/external confusion or a loss of ego boundaries. Taken on face value, the expression "ego-boundary confusion" suggests that subjects fail to recognize that inserted thoughts belong to or occur within the boundaries of their own egos or selves. It suggests that subjects regard the relevant thoughts as external to themselves, even as falling within the boundaries of another person's ego. So interpreted, delusions or experiences of thought insertion involve a subject's being introspectively aware of a thought while regarding it as external to herself. If that is the case, then delusions of thought insertion provide empirical evidence against the thesis that introspective awareness necessarily involves self attribution—a thesis that enjoys a distinguished philosophical pedigree, although it is a topic of fierce contention among philosophers.

We shall show that the above face-value understanding of thought insertion is mistaken and that, once the mistake is recognized, thought insertion turns out to be irrelevant to whether introspection requires self attribution. In exposing the mistake, we lead the reader through a process of trial and error by which we come to understand the need to distinguish a sense of "mine" in which I can acknowledge that a thought occurs in me and is mine but deny that it is *my* thought, something that *I* think.

6.2 What Is Thought Insertion?

Thought insertion may be, after verbal hallucinations, the most extensively discussed "positive" symptom of schizophrenia. It sits on Schneider's (1959) influential list of "first rank" symptoms of schizophrenia. One careful survey of the relative frequency of psychotic symptoms found that it occurs in 52 percent of patients diagnosed with schizophrenia (Sartorius et al. 1977).

Fish's Schizophrenia (1962/1984), a standard clinical handbook, characterizes thought insertion as follows:

Thinking, like all conscious activities, is experienced as an activity which is being carried on by the subject. . . . There is a quality of "my-ness" connected with thought. In schizophrenia this sense of the possession of one's thoughts may be impaired and the patient may suffer from alienation of thought. . . . [The patient] is certain that alien thoughts have been inserted in his mind. (p. 48)

Frith (1992, p. 66) quotes one patient's account:

Thoughts are put into my mind like "Kill God." It is just like my mind
working, but it isn't. They come from this chap, Chris. They are his
thoughts.

Mellor (1970, p. 17) quotes a particularly vivid patient report:

I look out the window and I think that the garden looks nice and the
grass looks cool, but the thoughts of Eamonn Andrews come into my
mind. There are no other thoughts there, only his. . . . He treats my mind
like a screen and flashes thoughts onto it like you flash a picture.

   Cases of thought insertion appear patently bizarre: a thought
in me and introspected by me, but which I say is not mine? But
perhaps "thought insertion" is a misnomer, a metaphorical
description of a more prosaic sort of experience. Perhaps Mellor's
patient merely is giving emphatic expression to the belief that
Eamonn Andrews (a British TV personality) has undue or unusual
influence over her thinking. The thoughts in question are
Andrews's only in the sense that they are thoughts that he wants
her to think or for which he is causally responsible for her thinking. We sometimes say that others have put ideas into our head
or that others have done our thinking for us. The use of these
familiar idioms does not mean that we believe that some episode
in our psychological history is, literally, another person's thought.
Indeed, it is not clear that it makes any logical sense to say that
an episode in one person's psychological history is some other
person's thought; hence the bizarreness.
   However, clinicians do tend to interpret reports of thought
insertion literally. Delusions of thought insertion are distinguished
from the belief, perhaps also delusory, that one's thinking has been
influenced by another. K. W. M. Fulford (1989, p. 221) writes:

The normal experience of one's own thoughts being influenced is like thought insertion to the extent that it is . . . something that is "done or happens" to one. But the similarity is only superficial. For in the normal case, that which is being done or is happening to one is simply the *influencing* of one's thoughts; whereas in the case of thought insertion it is (bizarrely) the thinking itself.

A popular textbook (Fish 1962/1985, p. 49) notes:

In thought-alienation [i.e., thought insertion] the patient has the experience that . . . others are participating in his thinking. He feels that thoughts are being inserted into his mind and he recognizes them as foreign and coming from without.

Wing (1978, p. 105) remarks:

The symptom is not that [the patient] has been caused to have unusual thoughts . . . but [that] the thoughts *themselves* are not his.

Sims (1995, p. 154) emphasizes that, although both thought influence and thought insertion are "passivity" experiences, it is important to distinguish between them; they are not one and the same clinical phenomenon.

Thus, the clinical consensus is that patients suffering from delusions of thought insertion do mean to assert that the relevant thoughts are somebody's else's thoughts and not the patient's own. But how can the patient mean to say something like this, and does it make any sense (even by standards of schizophrenic symptomatology)?

6.3 Thought Insertion and Ego-Boundary Confusion

Somebody else's thoughts in me: what does that mean, literally?

Sims (1995, p. 152) describes the disturbance of self-consciousness in thought insertion by reference to the ability to discern "the boundary between what is self and what is not self":

In thought insertion [the subject] experiences thoughts that do not have the feeling of being his own, but he feels that they have been put in his mind without his volition, from the outside. As in thought withdrawal, there is clearly a disturbance of self-image, and especially in the boundary between what is self and what is not.

This account suggests that the subject mislocates the inserted thought relative to the self/nonself boundary, taking it to lie outside rather than within the boundary. And Sims enjoys famous company. Freud (1962, p. 13) also insisted that people are capable of such boundary errors:

Pathology has made us acquainted with a great number of states in which the boundary lines between the ego and the external world become uncertain or in which they are actually drawn incorrectly. There are cases in which part of a person's own body, even portions of his mental life— his perceptions, thoughts, and feelings—appear alien to him and as not belonging to his own ego.

Freud surely is right about a person's sense of the boundary of his body. One can experience parts of one's own body as something alien. Some years ago a paper with the fascinating title "Self-shooting of a phantom head" appeared in the *British Journal of Psychiatry* (Ames 1984). The paper described the case of a patient who attempted to shoot a head attached between his shoulders, which he maintained was the head of his wife's gynecologist. He suspected the doctor of seducing his wife, and he claimed that the head spoke with the doctor's voice. The patient shot himself several times through the palate, causing extensive though not immediately fatal brain damage.

But what about conscious mental life? What about thought insertion? Does it reflect boundary confusion?

If the literal loss-of-ego-boundary story provides the proper understanding of the alien character of inserted thoughts (i.e., if the subject takes them to occur outside her ego boundary rather than within it), then thought insertion has important implications for the study of human self-consciousness. Presumably the subject is aware of her inserted thoughts introspectively, just as she is aware of her "normal" thoughts. However, if she regards them as literally alien, as occurring external to her, then it would seem that her introspective awareness of an episode in her own mental life or psychological history does not involve her being aware of it as an episode in her mental life. It would seem that she somehow conceives of the thought as taking place outside her.

Remember that subjects caught up in delusions of thought insertion are supposed to regard their inserted thoughts as foreign and alien, not merely as under alien influence. They attribute the thoughts to other persons, to "Chris" or "Eamonn Andrews."

John Locke, in his *Essay Concerning Human Understanding*, wrote of "it being impossible for anyone to perceive without perceiving that he does perceive." He continued: "When we see, hear, smell, taste, feel, mediate, or will anything, we know that we do so. Thus, it is always as to our present sensations and perceptions: and by this everyone is to himself that which he calls self." (1959, p. 449) Here Locke is asserting that my awareness of my own mental activities or of my own thoughts necessarily involves awareness of them as my own. At least this much of Locke's psychological theory has been endorsed by latter-day students of self-consciousness, including Roderick Chisholm (1976) and Sydney Shoemaker (1986). Shoemaker holds that we are so constituted that our being in certain sorts of mental states directly produces in us beliefs to the effect that *we* are in the states. This, he says, is what our introspective access to our own mental activities

amounts to. He describes as "indefensible" under any interpretation "the view that we have introspective perceptions of individual mental happenings but not of a self" (p. 117). Thus, from the
Locke-Chisholm-Shoemaker perspective, introspective awareness
of a thought necessarily involves awareness that it belongs to or
falls within the borders of one's own self or ego. Hereafter we
shall refer to introspective awareness that a thought falls within
one's own self or ego as awareness of the *subjectivity* of a
thought.

The Lockean tradition is opposed by an equally distinguished tradition concerning the relation between introspection
and awareness of subjectivity. David Hume, in the *Treatise*,
famously insisted that when he entered most intimately (introspectively) into himself he encountered only particular impressions and ideas, not a self in whom those ideas occurred (Hume
1978, p. 252). C. S. Peirce (1934) and Bertrand Russell (1981)
likewise affirmed that we may be aware of various episodes in our
mental lives without thereby recognizing them as episodes in our
mental lives.

A latter-day representative of the Humean tradition, D. M.
Armstrong (1968, p. 337), maintains that, although introspection
(which Armstrong calls "inner sense") reveals to us our current
mental activities, "all that inner sense reveals is the occurrence of
individual mental happenings." The subjectivity of those mental
happenings is not observed by inner sense. Rather, Armstrong
says, we "postulate" the existence of a subject. This postulate is a
"theoretical construct" that serves to explain apparent connections among the happenings presented to us in introspection.
Apprehension of self requires a hypothetical inference that goes
"beyond what is introspectively observed" (ibid., p. 337). Since

introspective awareness *per se* of individual mental happenings requires no such inference, we can readily understand why introspection does not suffice for *self* consciousness. One can be aware of a mental happening and yet fail to endorse or even to entertain the hypothesis that this happening occurs in oneself. Awareness of a thought need not involve awareness of its subjectivity.

Armstrong speculates that a subject might find a particular mental happening so "alien" with respect to other mental episodes he has introspectively observed that he "forms the hypothesis that it is not a state of [the same self] of which the other members are states" (ibid., p. 338). Armstrong imagines such a person saying to himself "It is not I, but something alien." Although mentioned only as a theoretical possibility, Armstrong's case sounds very like an experience of thought insertion. The subject says to herself "This isn't my *thought*: it isn't part of my psychological history: it doesn't occur within the boundaries of me: it is Mr. Andrews's thought, and it belongs to him."

Following the account sketched by Armstrong, we can say that in order to recognize a thought as *mine*, to recognize its subjectivity, I must realize that it occurs within the boundary of my self: that it belongs to the series of mental happenings that constitute my psychological history. On the Armstrongian view, the boundaries of this self are not visible to me in introspection. Rather, their location must be inferred from the characteristics of the mental happenings. This suggests the possibility of mislocating the boundary, excluding things that actually occur inside it or including things that fall outside it. Delusions of thought insertion, then, would represent errors of exclusion. The Armstrongian subject discovers a thought by introspection, but she fails to correctly locate it within her ego boundaries. Instead, she regards it as something outside the boundary, perhaps even as belonging to someone else.

Things seem to be in place for an ego-boundary-confusion description of thought insertion. Armstrong's account of self-consciousness provides a conceptual context for understanding what is going on in thought insertion. Meanwhile, the phenomenon of thought insertion provides Armstrong with evidence that introspective awareness (inner sense) without awareness of subjectivity is more than a mere theoretical possibility. The phenomenon challenges Shoemaker's contention that introspection necessarily involves the subject's belief that she introspects an activity of herself.

So things seem, but that is not how they are. In the examples of thought insertion discussed in the clinical literature, patients are well aware of the subjectivity of their thoughts: of where they occur. They regard them as occurring within their ego boundaries. The patient quoted by Frith says "Thoughts are put into my mind." Mellor's patient doesn't speak of perceiving thoughts occurring outside her mind; rather, she accuses Eamonn Andrews of putting his thoughts into *her* mind: "He treats my mind like a screen and flashes thoughts onto it like you flash a picture." (Mellor 1970, p. 17) Whatever these patients are deluded about, they are not confused about where the alien thoughts occur. They locate them correctly within the boundaries of their own minds or psychological histories. Shoemaker may not be vindicated by patient reports, but he is not challenged.

Clinical accounts of thought insertion emphasize that the subject has the sense that another person *intervenes* in the subject's mind: that another person somehow carries out his own thinking within the subject's psychological history. The subject regards the thoughts as alien not because she supposes that they occur outside her, but in spite of her awareness that they occur within her. Her distress arises not (as Freud or Sims would have it) from loss of ego boundaries and uncertainty about whether things are inside or outside the boundary, but from her sense that her ego boundary has been violated and that something alien has been placed within it.

Whatever its merits as a general theory of subjectivity, Armstrong's account does not give us the conceptual resources for understanding thought insertion. Armstrong claims that we need to explain how I recognize that a thought of which I am introspectively aware occurs in me, that I am its subject. If he is right, whatever explains the alien character of inserted thoughts lies in a conceptual or epistemic space between my introspective awareness of a thought and my conclusion that the thought occurs in my psychological history. In contrast, whatever explains the alien character of inserted thoughts, as reported in the clinical literature, does not inhabit that space. Persons suffering from delusions of thought insertion realize that inserted thoughts occur in their mind. They grasp their subjectivity; if there is an inference that a thought of which one is introspectively aware occurs in one's psychological history, this inference has already occurred. Nevertheless, and here is the conceptual oddity of thought insertion, subjects deny that they think the relevant thoughts. They insist that the thought is not theirs but another's, despite their recognition of its subjectivity. Thus, the question that is relevant for thought insertion is this: What remains to be explained about my awareness that a thought is my own, once we explain how I recognize that the thought occurs in me? The existence of delusions of thought insertion shows that something remains to be explained. Explaining how we recognize the subjectivity of our thoughts does not resolve the question of how we recognize that they are our own, that we *think* them.

If the sense of subjectivity is not the problem in thought insertion, what is? Before plunging into our own attempt to explain the sort of alienation involved in thought insertion, we wish to spend a few more moments on the topic of ego-boundary confusion.

6.4   Boundary Confusion and Multiple Personality Disorder

Does the psychopathology literature contain any clear-cut cases of ego-boundary confusion—cases in which the subject takes her own mental activities to occur externally to her, in somebody else's consciousness or psychological history?

We know of only one sort of case that might fit the bill. This is a phenomenon alleged to occur in multiple personality disorder (also known as dissociative identity disorder). Patients with MPD exhibit what are called "alters" (short for "alternate personalities"). Typically, from the outside, alters are considered to be functionally distinct states of a single psychological organism, or "roles" played by a single subject. A subject may, for example, have an alter called Cordelia. As Cordelia, the subject expresses love and respect for her father and remembers many pleasant interactions with him. The same subject has another alter, however: Regan. In her Regan mode, she expresses hatred and contempt for her father. Different sorts of epistemic access relations may hold, or fail to hold, between Cordelia and Regan. Cordelia may be unaware of Regan's existence, for example, while Regan claims to know all about Cordelia. Or Cordelia might claim to know what Regan does, but not what Regan thinks. If Regan and Cordelia comment on each other, each will deny being the other and each will discuss the other's traits from a third-person or spectatorial point of view.

Suppose that we (the clinical "we") know or assume that the same subject is speaking whether she speaks as Cordelia or Regan (although we may debate just what it means to be the same subject in this context—see Flanagan 1994 and Graham 1999a,b). When Regan contrasts herself with Cordelia, disowning Cordelia's actions and attitudes, let us suppose that the subject is, in her current state, dissociating herself from features of her own psychological history. Thus, when Regan says that Cordelia loves her father but that she (Regan) "hates the bastard," we view this as the subject's temporarily denying her own affection for her father.

Consider a few clinical examples of one alter commenting on another:

"Joy is happy and playful, so sometimes when I'm down . . . she becomes me. Sometimes it cheers me up, but sometimes it is only Joy who is happy and I'm still upset." (Bliss 1986, p. 231)

Therapist: "What are the feelings she has trouble with?"
Patient: "Getting mad. She can't get mad."
Therapist: "She can't get mad, but you can?"
Patient: "Oh, yes. I get furious. But she can't get mad." (Confer and Ables 1983, p. 121)

If alters are not in fact distinct persons sharing a single body, but are one and the same person, the speaker in each of the above cases is describing her own feelings and behavior. She is referring to her own playfulness, her own inability to get angry on occasion. These descriptions may quite accurately describe her attitudes and conduct during those periods when the relevant alter is manifest. Nevertheless, she ascribes these traits to another person, not to herself.

Now, MPD cases may seem to show that, on reflection, a subject can come to view what are in fact features of her own psychological history as subjectively alien: as having occurred not in her, but in someone else's psychological history. However, we must be careful here, for this is not exactly what Armstrong is looking for. Locke and Shoemaker don't deny that we can fail to *remember* things we did and thought as features of our own psychological history. Nor do they deny that we can decide, after the fact, that somebody else must have done and thought those things. What they claim, against the Hume-Armstrong view, is that one cannot be introspectively (immediately, directly) aware of episodes in one's mental life and, simultaneously, regard them as something alien: something external to or outside the boundaries of one's mental life and part of another person or agent.

What the Armstrongian or ego-boundary-confusion view needs is an example of someone, so to speak, introspectively staring a thought in the face while thinking "This is no thought of mine; it's not really happening in me." Alters sometimes report having such experiences, and some theorists are prepared to take them seriously. Eddy Zemach (1986, p. 126) remarks that "in some cases of dissociation both subjects report being conscious at the same time." An alter will claim to have been "looking on" or "listening in" while another alter has control of the body (ibid.). Kathleen Wilkes (1988, p. 125) describes what she calls "intraconsciousness" among different alters as follows:

We should observe that Miss Beauchamp's plurality was not only diachronic—Sally, B1, and B4 by turns—but also synchronic. For whenever B1, B2, and B4 were in control, Sally coexisted as a second consciousness, aware of all their actions, and the thoughts at least of B1 and B2, while keeping her own counsel. Her consciousness was substantially independent of that of the personality in charge of the body at the time. . . . Sally observed, as an amused spectator, B1's dreams, even being able to give a fuller account of them than B1.

If intra-conscious or co-conscious episodes really occur, then we can imagine Sally simultaneously "observing" what B1 dreams or thinks and saying to herself: "I'm not dreaming that dream or thinking these thoughts. They're B1's mental occurrences, not my own." Then, if Sally and B1—despite their high degree of functional independence—are simply states of the same person or subject (Miss Beauchamp), Sally's comments reflect an experience of "subjective alienation." That is, she is introspectively conscious of a thought, and at the same instant she regards that thought as something occurring outside her ego or boundary (and in another). She is aware of a thought without recognizing its subjectivity. Or so some might argue.

However, there are at least two reasons for doubting that the sorts of cases described above constitute genuine examples of subjective alienation (ego-boundary confusion combined with ascription to another). First, if Sally and B1 are *that* functionally distinct, arguably they really should be described as separate subjects or persons. Sally is not one and the same person as B1.[1] Moreover, if Sally is a different subject or person from B1, then she is not deluded when she denies that those are her dreams and her thoughts. She is perfectly correct. Of course, we are then confronted with the question of whether her access to those thoughts

---

1. This is Zemach's (1986) conclusion.

(B1's thoughts) is introspective. If it is, then, contrary to usual or common-sense assumptions, subjects can have introspective access to other people's thoughts. This would vindicate the Armstrongian idea that introspection and awareness of subjectivity can come apart. Indeed, it would do so in a more dramatic manner than anything Armstrong himself had in mind, for it would allow us to enter, literally, into another person's stream of consciousness and observe events in that stream, as it were, firsthand. It would then be up to us to somehow infer which subject—whose stream—it is. On the other hand, one might deny that Sally (since, by hypothesis, she is a different person) is introspectively aware of B1's thoughts, assuming that, whether the subject realizes it or not, introspection *per se* can give access only to one's own thoughts. (The notion that introspection gives a person access only to his or her own thoughts is reinforced by talking of introspection as *inner* sense, that is, as the perception of episodes within one's own self.) However, in that case, Sally's experiences are not relevant to the Locke-Shoemaker thesis.

Rather than speculate about how to resolve the above issues, we shall point out a second problem associated with conceiving of MPD as evidence of the possibility of ego-boundary confusion. Experiences of co-consciousness or intra-consciousness are reported, of course, only in retrospect. Sally claims that she *was* conscious of B1's dreams, not that she *is* conscious of them. She claims that, even though she was not "out" at the time, she was still there and was aware of what was happening. Is this a report of a previous experience of co-consciousness, or is it an *ex post facto* reconstruction or confabulation by Sally of what she ought to have experienced had she been (contrary to psychological fact) co-conscious with B1? It seems difficult to be confident that the former is true. Shoemaker may insist, in a suspicious mood, that we lack sufficient grounds for proclaiming the reality of co-consciousness, and hence that we do not have a clinically secure counterexample to the thesis that introspection necessarily involves awareness of subjectivity.

This is where we must leave things. MPD is fascinating, but our interest is in thought insertion, not in multiple personality, which carries with it its own package of controversies (Spanos 1996). Clearly thought insertion is not an instance of subjective alienation. It is not a case of introspection minus awareness of subjectivity. Whether there are instances of such a phenomenon (say, in MPD) we are content to leave an open question. Clearly some sort of alienation is present in thought insertion. Precisely what is present, if not *subjective* alienation, is not yet clear.

6.5 Frith as Motetus

All this talk of voices and thought insertion makes us think of motets. Medieval motets typically occur in three voice parts, known as *tenor*, *motetus*, and *triplum*. Thus far, the main voice in the polyphony of this book has been that of Ralph Hoffman, though various chanters, including Marcel Kinsbourne, D. M. Armstrong, and others have been heard. If we are to have genuine polyphony, we need other voices. For motetus we turn to Christopher Frith.

Frith (1992) no longer endorses the input account of voices discussed in chapter 4 above. His new approach to explaining experiences of alienation within disturbances of self-consciousness has several attractive features from our point of view.

(1)   Frith recognizes that in some experiences conventionally regarded as verbal or auditory hallucinations "there is no sensory

component" (ibid., p. 77). In those cases, and perhaps others, the alien quality of the voice must be accounted for without falling back on the notion that the subject confuses his awareness of his own inner speech with a perception of somebody else's speech.

(2) Frith appreciates that there is an affinity between verbal hallucinations and what he calls "passivity experiences":

> If hallucinations are caused by inner speech, then the problem is not that inner speech is occurring, but that the patient must be failing to recognize that this activity is self-initiated. The patient misattributes self-generated actions to an external agent. . . . There are a number of other positive symptoms of schizophrenia that explicitly concern the attribution of the patient's own actions to outside agents. These are the so-called "passivity experiences": thought insertion and delusions of control. (ibid., p. 73)

Frith attempts to give a unified account of verbal hallucinations and passivity experiences, including thought insertion.

(3) Frith's unified account, like Hoffman's and like the one we will offer in chapter 8, is developed by emphasizing the action-like features of thought and inner speech and by appealing to the notion—familiar from Hoffman—that we may experience our thinking and our inner speaking as intended or unintended.

It is important for us to describe Frith's account and to distinguish it from our own.

Frith lays out his account of alienation in at least three places. The earliest is his paper "The positive and negative symptoms of schizophrenia reflect impairments in the perception and initiation of action," published in *Psychological Medicine* in 1987. The second is a co-authored paper in the *British Journal of Psychiatry* titled "Towards a neuropsychiatry of schizophrenia" (Frith and Done 1988). Third, the view is set out in relevant sections of Frith's book *The Cognitive Neuropsychiatry of Schizophrenia* (1992). There are subtle differences and changes in terminology among these three sources. We shall rely on the account in Frith 1992 for our basic presentation of his view, drawing on the other papers to clarify specific points of interpretation.

Frith develops his account of alienation in the context of a general theory of how and why people monitor their own mental activity. He describes voices, thought insertion, and so forth as breakdowns or failures of our monitoring of ourselves. Thus, the first task confronting an expositor is to explain his account of self-monitoring.

Frith begins by observing that it is important for us to discriminate between changes in our perceptual experience brought about by our own actions and changes "due to external events" (1992, p. 81). His favorite example concerns changes in our visual experience of the world brought about by our own eye or head movements and changes due to movements of objects in the environment. Knowing whether the visual scene has changed (i) because we are looking at it from different perspectives or sampling different portions of the scene or (ii) because something in the environment is moving relative to us is important for appropriately adjusting our behavior to the environment. We keep track of the origin of such perceptual changes by monitoring the movements of our eyes.

Eye monitoring is done by a cognitive system that is sensitive to "corollary discharge" associated with neurological commands or signals that initiate eye movements. When a change in the pattern of retinal stimulation is accompanied by detection of corollary discharge, the visual system automatically compensates and the positions of objects in the environment appear to remain fixed. If no corollary discharge accompanies a change in retinal stimulation, then external objects appear to shift their positions.

We know that it is corollary discharge from neural commands rather than the eye movements themselves that controls the visual compensation, because when the eyes are moved without appropriate neural signals (e.g., by pushing the eyeball with one's fingers) the external world appears to move or shift. Likewise, experiments in which an eye is paralyzed with curare and the subject attempts to move the eye (i.e. generates appropriate neural signals to initiate eye movements, which then generate the usual corollary discharge associated with eye movement) show that, again, the external scene appears to shift despite the fact that the pattern of retinal stimulation remains unchanged (since the eye didn't actually move). The explanation for this is that the brain has already compensated for the expected movement and, hence, the unchanged retinal image is interpreted as a shift of external objects in the direction of the expected eye movement. Objects seem to be moving so as to stay in front of the eye (Frith 1987).

Frith supposes that comparable or analogous sorts of monitoring keyed to internal (purportedly neurological) changes that normally accompany action enable us to distinguish in other cases between changes in our experience of the world that result from our own actions and changes due to alterations in the external environment. "A similar mechanism for monitoring all our actions," he writes, "would be a great importance for interpreting our perception of change." (1992, p. 81)

Frith presents evidence that schizophrenics deprived of observable feedback have difficulty determining whether they have acted (Frith 1992, pp. 82–83; Frith 1987, pp. 645–646; Frith and Done 1988, p. 440; Mlakar et al. 1994, pp. 557–564). That is, they have difficulty distinguishing, from the inside, whether a change in perceptual experience arises from their own actions or is brought about by external agencies. Frith proposes that this difficulty is due to their failure to centrally monitor their own actions.

Frith believes that auditory hallucinations can be attributed to monitoring failures. Confronted with an experience of speech, the subject cannot tell whether he generated the speech he experiences, either vocally or subvocally, or whether he is perceiving speech generated by someone else. Thus, he may interpret his experience of his own inner or subvocal speech as the auditory perception of another's speech. This is what is going on in "auditory" hallucinations—verbal hallucinations that have a genuine auditory component.[2] Frith (1992, p. 82) writes:

If we could not distinguish between events caused by our own actions and those of external origin, then we might attribute events caused by our own actions to external events. . . . One manifestation of this effect would be auditory hallucinations. The patient hears a voice and does not recognize it as their own.

What of thought insertion and instances of verbal hallucination that lack sensory components? Here Frith (1992, p. 81) invokes a second level of monitoring:

It is not only monitoring of actions that is impaired in schizophrenia. In addition, it is the monitoring of the intentions to act. I am essentially describing two steps in a central monitoring system. First, the relationship between actions and external events are [*sic*] monitored in order to distinguish between events caused by our own actions and by external agencies. This enables us to know about the causes of events. Second,

2. On p. 439 of Frith and Done 1988, the presumption is that such hallucinations involve the production of *audible* subvocal speech.

intentions are monitored in order to distinguish between actions caused by our own goals and plans (willed actions) and actions that are in response to external events (stimulus-driven actions). Such monitoring is essential if we are to have some awareness of the causes of our actions.

How do breakdowns at this second stage of monitoring give rise to experiences of passivity such as thought insertion? Here we need to look more closely at Frith's account of what happens when the subject undergoes delusions of thought insertion.

Frith (1992, p. 80) observes that "thought insertion, in particular, is an experience that is difficult to understand." The patient claims that thoughts that are not her own are coming into her head. That we humans can have such experiences, Frith says, "implies that we have some way of recognizing our own thoughts. It is as if each thought has a label on it saying 'mine.' If the labeling process goes wrong, then the thought would be perceived as alien. . . . This idea may sound fanciful when applied to thoughts." (ibid., pp. 80–81)

What is fanciful about this? Frith and Done (1988, p. 438) describe thought insertion as a "strikingly odd concept." They phrase the oddness or fancifulness as follows: Since all of our thoughts "are internally generated," there is "no possibility of having thoughts other than our own." What, then, could be the point of a monitoring system that keeps track of whether a thought occurring in my mind, presented to me in introspection, is *my* thought rather than someone else's thought? We are never confronted with the fundamental attribution problem of having to sort out our own thoughts from other people's thoughts. (Contrast this with the genuine problem of distinguishing visual perceptual changes due to our own actions from those due to external events.) Thus, a system that labeled thoughts as "mine" or "not mine" would seem *ad hoc* at best. Our only reason for supposing such a system to operate in us would be to explain delusions of thought insertion by invoking breakdown in the system.

So Frith supposes that the relevant thought-monitoring system does not, in fact, have the function of sorting my thoughts from other people's thoughts. Instead, what the system monitors is whether a given thought is intended or "willed" by me, stemming from my own goals and plans, or whether the thought occurs as a response to some external event (is "stimulus driven"). Why do I need to distinguish willed from stimulus-driven thoughts? Frith explains this in terms of a general need to distinguish actions brought about by one's own will, self-initiated actions, from actions that are in response to environmental events.

Philosophers may wonder about the cogency or the tenability of Frith's distinction between willed and stimulus-driven actions. Actions *per se* may seem willed, though they may form two classes (self-initiated and stimulus-responsive). Philosophical scruples about terminology aside, there is an interesting distinction here. Frith cites a considerable body of evidence that our ability to initiate an action (e.g., deciding to pick up a ball) and our ability to react to an immediate external stimulus (e.g., catching a ball thrown at one's face) as well as our ability to control a sequence of actions (e.g., walking a straight line) without and with external guidance (e.g., walking a line without a marker to follow versus following a line painted on the floor) are distinct in some important ways. These abilities can be differentially affected by pathologies (such as Parkinson's Disease) and seem to involve different regions of the brain (Frith and Done 1988, pp. 438–442; Frith 1987, pp. 641–643).

Frith proposes that the ability to monitor intentions to act allows us to correct erroneous responses rapidly, without having to wait for visual feedback. For example, normal subjects instructed to trace a shape on a computer screen using a joystick can detect and correct mistakes without having to see the screen. Schizophrenics correct such errors as competently as control subjects do when allowed to see the results of their joystick manipulations on the screen. However, when deprived of visual feedback, controls make rapid error corrections, whereas schizophrenics do not. Further, Frith (1992, pp. 82–83) notes that "this disability was restricted to patients with passivity experiences." "These results," he concludes (p. 83), "confirm that there is an impairment of self-monitoring: this impairment would lead to lack of awareness of their intended actions and could underlie some of the abnormal experiences of schizophrenic patients."

So, according to Frith, we all have a system for monitoring whether our actions, overt or covert (mental), result from our intentions (wills), as opposed to being stimulus driven. In schizophrenia this system is impaired, with the result that the subject experiences his own intended (willed) actions as if they come about as a result of forces outside or independent of his control:

How could failure of central monitoring give rise to schizophrenia symptoms? I have suggested . . . that a failure to monitor intentions to act would result in delusions of control and other passivity experiences. Thinking, like all our actions, is normally accompanied by a sense of effort and deliberate choice as we move from one thought to the next. If we found ourselves thinking without any awareness of the sense of effort that reflects central monitoring, we might well experience these thoughts as alien and, thus, being inserted into our minds. (Frith 1992, p. 81)

As in Hoffman, Frith's account of alienation assigns a crucial role to the subject's impression that he or she does not intend to produce the alien thought. But Hoffman and Frith offer different explanations of how the subject comes by this impression.

Hoffman argues that defective discourse planning produces unintended thoughts which the subject recognizes as such. Frith suggests that the relevant thoughts are intended but that a failure of monitoring prevents the subject from recognizing them as intended. However, in both accounts, the subject's sense or feeling that she did not intend to think a given thought, *t*, starts her down the road to the conclusion that *t* is attributable to someone else. Frith recognizes, moreover, that Hoffman's story about how the subject gets from her impression that she doesn't intend to think *t* to the conclusion that *t* is alien will not do for thought insertion and nonauditory voices. Unfortunately, Frith's own account fails to provide an alternative explanation for the route from feelings of unintendedness brought about by monitoring failure to the sort of experience of alienation found in thought insertion and in voices.

First, Frith does not explain why the subject of an inserted thought would take his thinking to be controlled by some outside agent rather than merely supposing that his thinking is unintended or stimulus driven. Presumably, schizophrenics and others have experience with unintended "actions" generally and with unintended thinking. Frith supposes that some of our thinking is stimulus driven: the point of his second monitoring system is precisely to help us to sort out willed from unintended actions. So, if my monitoring system reports that I'm engaged in a mental action and fails to detect any intention of mine controlling this action, the natural expectation would seem to be that I'd interpret the action as unintended. I would classify it as a response to some environmental stimulus. However, although this conclusion may be false, it's a long way from the delusion that some *other*

person is causing me to think the relevant thoughts: that the
thinking is inserted. Frith (1992, p. 81) covers this by saying
that "we might well experience these thoughts as alien." We
might well so experience the thought, but why do we sometimes
experience it as alien, why not experience it merely as
unintended?

Second, and relatedly, Frith gives us no clue as to why a
person might experience thought insertion, as opposed merely to
a delusion of being controlled by another (or of thought influence). As we have noted, thought insertion involves more than
merely supposing that another agent has influenced, or caused,
one's thinking; it involves the impression that a thought occurring in one's own stream of consciousness actually is someone
else's thinking. As Frith notes, this is an odd thing for someone
to believe. It is markedly odder than believing that another person
is somehow influencing or directing our thinking. To arrive at the
belief that another person's thoughts are occurring in her mind,
a subject would seem to need more to go on than her impression that she didn't intend to think the relevant thoughts.
However, on our reading, Frith has no story to tell about how
failing to detect an intention in connection with a particular
episode of thinking leads the subject to regard the episode as
something inserted into her mind by another person and, actually, as a episode of the other person's thinking rather than her
own. Though his account suggests that we might initially mark
inserted thoughts as deviant because of their apparent unintendedness, it falls short of explaining the full-blown experience of
alienation involved in delusions of thought insertion.

Frith aims for an account that explains not only thought
insertion and voices but also other experiences of "passivity." This
laudable search for generality may be responsible for his failure to

fully appreciate the peculiar problems presented by the first two phenomena. Although Frith comments on the oddity of the "concept" of thought insertion, he never comes to grips with it. The subject acknowledges that the alien thought occurs in her mind, but insists that it is someone else's thought. Is this an intelligible supposition? How can a thought in *her* mind be someone else's thought? In what sense does she take the thought to be alien?

Hoffman, at least, offers a coherent story about the experience of alienation of verbal hallucinations: The subject takes herself to be hearing another's overt speech. The experience of the voice is alien in the sense that it is supposed to be an experience of something external to her, the other's speech act. She does not regard the inner-speech episode that constitutes the voice as itself something alien. Rather, she regards it as her own perceptual experience and recognizes its subjectivity.

Frith realizes that no such account is available for a subject's experience of inserted thoughts or nonauditory voices. This is because in those phenomena what the subject takes to be alien is an episode in her own stream of consciousness, her own psychological history. It is the episode itself, not its object, that she attributes to another. However, Frith never explains how the subject can both correctly locate the episode within her ego boundaries and believe that it is someone else's thought. Frith may assume that his comparison between thought insertion and experiences of alien influence or control helps resolve this explanatory problem. He may suppose that the subject takes the relevant thoughts to be alien in the sense that they are under another's control rather than her own control. However, this still leaves an explanatory problem. Thought insertion is one thing; thought influence is something else.

According to conventional clinical wisdom, a subject's experience of alienation in thought insertion differs from the experience of alienation in delusions of influence. Does Frith dispute the conventional understanding? He takes note of the standard distinction (1992, p. 66; see also Frith and Done 1988, p. 439), but he never makes his own response to it explicit. The tone of his discussion suggests that he also regards thought insertion as something distinct from delusions of influence. However, if Frith accepts the conventional distinction, he needs to account for what is distinctive about the experience of alienation in thought insertion. Moreover, no matter how he views the relation between thought insertion and experiences of influence, Frith needs to explain how the subject's having the impression that she did not intend to think a certain thought leads her to the hypothesis that someone else thinks or causes her to think that thought.

To satisfactorily come to grips with the conceptual and explanatory problems regarding introspective alienation, we need (to continue with the metaphor of the motet) a third voice.

Our triplum is Harry Frankfurt.

7

In the Frankfurt School

7.1 Frankfurtian Externality

In *The Importance of What We Are About*, Harry Frankfurt describes a hypothetical incident in which a man, seized by a fit of anger, insults a companion and then, recovering his self-possession, pleads to be excused: "I have no idea what triggered the bizarre spasm of emotion. It came over me out of nowhere and I couldn't help it. I wasn't myself." (Frankfurt 1988, p. 63) Though allowing that such pleas may be insincere, Frankfurt holds that "It is also possible that they are genuinely descriptive." He continues:

What the man says may appropriately convey his sense that the rise of passion represented in some way an intrusion on him. . . . That when he was possessed by anger he was not in possession of himself. It is in statements like the ones made by the man in the example, and in the sense of self that such statements express, that we most vividly encounter the experience of externality.

Frankfurt is one of the most prominent contributors to the recent literature on free will.[1] He develops an account of the

---

1. For evidence of the prominence of Frankfurt's contribution, see Shatz 1986 and Kane 1996.

experience of externality in the context of traditional philosophical concerns about freedom and autonomy. However, he also insists on the importance of the notion for our understanding of human self-consciousness, remarking that the experience of externality "leads into the center of our experience of ourselves" (p. 59). It is in this connection that we shall discuss his view.

We should make clear at the outset that Frankfurt does not have in mind by "experiences of externality" experiences of alienation. He also does not have in mind such phenomena as thought insertion or voices. He develops his account without reference to psychopathology. We will be applying his ideas to problems he does not consider, and perhaps extending them in ways he would not approve. Nevertheless, we believe that Frankfurt has much to teach us about the experience of alienation. What he calls "experiences of externality" (hereafter "externalization" for short) present a conceptual problem that is very similar to the problem of how a subject undergoing delusions of thought insertion or verbal hallucination can maintain that a mental episode is another's thought while acknowledging that it occurs in her own mind. Frankfurt proposes a solution to the conceptual problem of externalization that, in our view, also suggests a solution to the conceptual problem presented by experiences of alienation, partly because it is at least a tacit assumption of an experience of alienation that it is also an experience of externality: an experience of not attributing, in some sense, to oneself.

7.2   The Conceptual Problem of Externalization

Although Frankfurt alludes to instances in which "we most vividly encounter the experience of externality," his presentation suffers from a notable deficiency of vivid, real-world examples of externalization. Oliver Sacks helps us to remedy this deficiency by recounting two striking experiences of externality in his auto-biographical book *A Leg to Stand On.* In the first experience, Sacks is dragging himself back down a mountain trail after having been seriously injured in a fall. At one point he stops, overcome by exhaustion:

"How nice it is here," I thought to myself. "Why not a little rest—a nap maybe?" The apparent sound of this soft, insinuating, inner voice suddenly woke me, sobered me, and filled me with alarm. It was not "a nice place" to rest and nap. The suggestion was lethal and filled me with horror . . . "No," I said fiercely to myself. "This is Death speaking and in its sweetest, deadliest Siren-voice. Don't listen to it now. Don't listen to it ever. You've got to go on." (Sacks 1984, p. 30)

Later, while convalescing, Sacks finds himself watching a school team practicing rugby:

I was surprised and appalled at the spasm of hate in myself. . . . I looked at them with the virulent envy, the mean rancor, the poisonous spite of the invalid; and then I turned away; I could bear them no longer. Nor could I bear my own feelings, the revealed ugliness in me. I consoled myself by saying, "This isn't me—the real me—but my sickness which is speaking." (ibid., pp. 176–177)

Sacks's experiences display the essential features of Frank-furtian experiences of externality. He acknowledges the occurrence of relevant mental episodes in himself—"I thought to myself," "a spasm of hate in myself"—but he also has the sense that, somehow, they are not attributable to himself—"This isn't me, not the real me."

Sacks also reports his sense of the "other self," of the alien or foreign character of the episodes, by attributing their occurrence to the operation of nonself agency within himself—"This is Death speaking," "my sickness which is speaking." Of course,

Sacks himself does not believe that the proposed Death and Sickness are real agents. He does not suffer from delusions of inserted thought. He experiences his thoughts as somehow not his own, but not as another's thoughts.

One might suppose that, despite Frankfurt's lack of attention to such cases, experiences involving alienation should also count as examples of what he calls "externalization."

Mellor (1970, p. 17) offers two vivid descriptions of alienated self-experience:

The patient experiences feelings which do not seem to be his own. The feelings are attributed to some external source and are imposed upon him. A 23-year-old female patient reported: "I cry, tears roll down my cheeks and I look unhappy, but inside I have a cold anger because they are using me in this way, and it is not me who is unhappy, but they are projecting unhappiness into my brain. . . . You have no idea how terrible it is to laugh and to look happy and to know that it is not you."

A 26-year-old patient emptied the contents of his urine bottle over the ward dinner trolley. He said, "The sudden impulse came over me that I must do it. It was not my feeling, it came into me from the x-ray department. . . . It was nothing to do with me, they wanted it done."

Although these cases raise the additional issue of attribution to another, in both situations the subject denies that an episode is attributable to herself or himself while acknowledging that the episode occurred in him or her. Since Frankfurt does not consider such cases, it is not clear whether he would recognize them as examples of "externalization."

Even without raising the issue of alienation, Sacks's experiences present a conceptual puzzle. He experiences the "inner voice," the "spasm of hate" as occurring within himself, yet he also feels that "This isn't me." But how can he have it both ways? If Sacks says this spasm of hate occurs in him but is not his, is there any way to interpret his statement literally without turning it into a contradiction? Suppose that Sacks sought to excuse his spitefulness by saying "This isn't me," as happens in Frankfurt's hypothetical example. Could his statement be "genuinely descriptive"? What sort of intelligible experience of self could it "appropriately convey"?

This is the conceptual problem or puzzle that confronts Frankfurt's notion of externalization. If a thought occurs in my mind, it would seem to follow, as a matter of logical necessity, that it is mine: my thought, my feeling. It would seem, then, that if I acknowledge the episode's innerness while denying that it is my thought then I must either be deeply confused or deviously insincere (Penelhum 1979). That a thought should be both an episode in my consciousness and not mine doesn't represent a coherent or intelligible content of experience. At least, so one might argue.

In response to this conceptual problem, Frankfurt insists that "it is not incoherent, despite the air of paradox, to say that a thought occurring in my mind may or may not be something *I think*" (1988, p. 59). He also makes the following assertions:

A person is no more to be identified with everything that goes on in his mind . . . than he is to be identified with everything that goes on in his body. Of course, every movement of a person's body is an event in his history: in this sense it is his and no one else's. In this same sense, all the events in the history of a person's mind are his too . . . But this is only a gross literal truth, which masks distinctions that are as valuable in the one case as they are in the other. (p. 61)

Let us see what Frankfurt has in mind here and then explore its application to experiences of externality. Frankfurt maintains that we can dispel the air of paradox that attaches to the idea that a thought occurring in my mind may not be (experienced as) mine by distinguishing two senses in which a thought may be said to be mine or not mine (i.e., internal or external to me). He introduces this distinction by way of an analogy to attributions of bodily movements to persons: I may acknowledge that, for example, my arm has gone up, but deny that I raised my arm. I may be either actively or passively involved in the movements at my body. Some bodily movements express my agency. Others do not, even though their causes may be internal to my body—a muscle spasm, for instance. Frankfurt observes that "we think it correct to attribute to a person, in the strict sense, only some of the events in the history of his body. The others—those with respect to which he is passive—have their moving principles outside him, and we do not identify him with these events." (p. 61) He admits that the relevant notions of passive and active involvement are difficult to make entirely precise, and that for certain purposes we may attribute events to a person even though their moving principles lie outside him. Frankfurt insists, however, that we recognize a distinction between what is attributable to the person "in the strict sense" and what is attributable to him merely in virtue of its having occurred "in the history of his body."

Frankfurt contends that the active/passive distinction extends to mental activities. I may be either active or passive with respect to my own thoughts and feelings. I may deliberately turn my ratiocination to a particular topic, as when I recite a poem silently to myself or when I mentally rehearse an argument. These are activities in which a person himself actively engages. However, it may also happen that thoughts come unbidden into my mind— a bit of doggerel runs through my head, or an advertising jingle recurs despite my efforts to distract myself. "The thoughts that beset us in these ways," Frankfurt writes, do not occur by our own active doing. It is tempting, indeed, to suggest that they are not thoughts that *we think* at all, but rather thoughts that we *find* occurring within us. This would express our sense that, although these thoughts are events in the histories of our minds, we do not actively participate in their occurrence. . . . A thought that occurs in my mind may or may not be something that *I think*. (p. 59)

Sacks acknowledges that spiteful thoughts occur in him, while denying that it is he who thinks or "speaks" them. Perhaps in this denial he lacks insight or honesty, but he does not contradict himself. He recognizes that he is the subject in whose psychological history the thought occurs, but refuses to attribute it to himself as the person or agent behind the thought. Frankfurt contends that resistance to personal self-attribution may be sincere and accurate and is not incoherent or unintelligible. Again: "A person is no more to be identified with everything that goes on in his mind . . . than he is to be identified with everything that goes on in his body." (p. 61)

Frankfurt does not assert that the internal-to-the-person/external-to-the-person distinction is exactly the same as the active/passive distinction. He suggests only that the two distinctions "are in certain respects analogous" (p. 68). What is at issue here is simply the coherence of the claim that a thought or a feeling occurring in my mind may fail to seem to be *my* thought or feeling. Frankfurt uses the analogy with the action theoretic active/passive distinction only to show that this claim can be coherent.

7.3   A Frankfurtian Concept of Alienation

Frankfurt's distinction between thoughts that I *think* and thoughts that I find occurring in me dovetails nicely with Hoffman's and

Frith's distinction between thoughts that I experience as intended by me and thoughts that strike me as unintended by me. According to Hoffman and Frith, my sense that I did not intend to think a particular thought is intimately tied up with my sense that this thought is not mine. This suggests that one might use a Frankfurt-style strategy to produce at least a partial solution to the conceptual problem regarding the experience of voices and inserted thoughts. (In order to absolve Frankfurt of any responsibility for what follows, we speak of a "Frankfurtian" and "Frankfurt-style" strategy, rather than "Frankfurt's strategy.")

We wish to introduce a distinction between two strands or components in a subject's experience of alienation—the externality impression that a thought is not the subject's own and the alienated impression that it is someone else's thought—without meaning that these impressions necessarily are introspectively separable in self-awareness. Concentrating for the moment on the first impression (that a thought is not the subject's own), we suggest that there are two ways in which a person might experience a thought as her own or not her own. First, she might experience the thought as belonging or as not belonging to her psychological history—i.e., as occurring within or outside her ego boundaries. We call this the sense of the *subjectivity* of the thought. Second, she might experience the thought as something that she *thinks* (i.e., as her own action or activity), as opposed to something that merely happens in her. We call this the sense of the *agency* of the thought.

Viewed in light of the sense of subjectivity/sense of agency distinction, the subject's assertion that a thought that occurs in her mind is not her own becomes intelligible. It makes sense conceptually. When she denies that the thought is her thought, she does not contradict the claim that it occurs in her. Rather, she may be interpreted as saying that, although the thought occurs in her, she does not regard herself as its agent or author. She admits to being the subject in whom the thought occurs, but denies that she *thinks* the thought.

We propose that the sense of agency and the sense of subjectivity represent distinct strands or components of self-consciousness, and that it is possible for these strands to unravel or break apart. More specifically, I may experience a thought as *subjectively* but not *agentically* my own. This possibility is realized in experiences of thought insertion and voices. Recognition of the distinction between the senses of subjectivity and agency helps to make the experiences intelligible.

The distinction between the sense of subjectivity and the sense of agency provides a partial solution to the problem of intelligibility for experiences of externality. It allows us to render intelligible the subject's assertion that a thought occurring in her mind is not something she thinks. However, we have yet to confront the problem for alienation proper: the assertion that a thought occurring in her mind is somebody else's thought. We can understand how I can coherently deny that a thought occurring in me is my thought. However, can we understand how I could insist that it is someone else's thought?

Frankfurt does not consider the possibility that one might attribute one's thought to another when he works out his account of the experience of externality, but his approach can be extended to cover the experience of alienation. On our view, my admitting that a thought occurred in my mind while denying that I think that thought is like my admitting that my arm went up but denying that I raised my arm. Similarly, admitting that a thought occurs in my mind while insisting that somebody else thinks that thought is like insisting that somebody else raised my arm. An episode in the history of my body might constitute something that somebody does even though it is not something that I do. Another person can raise my arm, by grasping my wrist and picking up my arm. In that case, raising my arm is his action, not mine. He is the agent who carries out the arm movement, even though the movement happened in or to my body.

Interestingly, there is a class of delusions whose salient feature is the subject's belief that other persons are the agents of his or her bodily movements. Mellor (1970, p. 18) quotes a patient's report:

When I reach for the comb it is my hand and arm which move. . . . But I don't control them. I sit watching them move and they are quite independent, what they do is nothing to do with me. I am just a puppet manipulated by cosmic strings.

Bliss (1986, p. 140) describes a patient who, "despondent and guilty on the anniversary of her mother's death, watched another personality put her arm in a fire. . . . The patient had no control over the movement and felt the pain as she watched the skin char."

We propose that experiences of thought insertion involve an analogous impression or belief concerning one's thoughts. The subject has the sense that a thought occurring in her mind has been carried out by or expresses the agency of another person. She attributes the "movement" of her mind to the other, saying that he is the person who has done or *thinks* it. She acknowledges her own involvement in this episode, but she sees herself not as the agent but only as the patient or subject in whom the thought occurs. No doubt her belief in another's agency is mistaken; our point is that it is not incoherent or unintelligible. The way in which she attributes the thought to herself is not the same as the way in which she attributes it to the other and denies that it is hers. Hence, her attributions may be taken literally and are mutually consistent. One attribution answers the question of who is the *subject* in which the thought occurs, and the other answers the question of who is the *agent* who carries out the thought.

K. W. M. Fulford has a nice way of summing up the understanding of experiences of alienation sketched above. He notes that a subject normally experiences her thoughts as things "done by" her. In thought insertion, she experiences them as things "done to" her by another (Fulford 1989, p. 221).

We are advocating here what may be called a breakdown-in-the-experience-of-agency model of the intelligibility of experiences of externality and alienation. We are saying that our sense of ourselves in self-consciousness actually is two senses: one of ourselves as subject, the other of ourselves as agent. On this model, in externality and alienation the sense of agency breaks apart from the sense of subjectivity. In alienation, in addition, the sense of agency places the agency in another.

We now have in place a conceptual framework for explicating the experience of alienation. In our final chapter, we apply this framework to the problem of understanding voices and thought insertion.

Alienated Self-Consciousness Explained

8.1 Framing the Explanation

A person's experience of alienation in voices or inserted thoughts represents a breakdown or disturbance in her sense of agency. How is this possible? When she reports that a thought occurring in her mind is not her own, but another's, she expresses her impression that another and not she herself is carrying out the thinking. However, what could lead a person to regard a thought occurring in her mind as a manifestation of somebody else's agency? What introspectively distinguishes those thoughts she recognizes as agentically her own from those she experiences as agentically alien?

We begin to answer this question by explicitly recognizing that, in asking how a person could regard an episode in her own mind as the manifestation of someone else's thinking, we do not pretend to explain why some individuals are more vulnerable than others to such experiences. Nor do we mean to explain why in some subjects alienation remains simply an occasional and anomalous "experience," while other people develop profound delusions. We also want to stress that what is wanted here, and what we propose, is not an account of what *makes* thoughts agentically one's own. In contrast to Hoffman (and perhaps to Frith), we neither need nor wish to commit ourselves to an account of the actual causal mechanics of thinking. We do not need to say things like "Some thoughts *are* intended while other thoughts are unintended." Perhaps, just perhaps, the sense of agency is groundless and our impression that some of our thoughts express our agency is a kind of user's illusion.

We are trying to tell a story about how introspective alienation works. Ours is an account of the *experience* of alienation. We need an account that is consistent with the clinical data and with otherwise plausible assumptions about human self-consciousness. Although our tale will leave unanswered various questions about the ultimate nature of agency in thinking, we don't see any way to make progress toward understanding voices and thought insertion except by attempting some such account.

8.2   Explaining Failure of Self-Attribution

As in our discussion in the preceding chapter of the conceptual problem of the experience of alienation, we shall first consider why a subject might feel that she is not the agent of a thought occurring in her stream of consciousness. We shall then turn to the question of alienation proper—that is, how she comes to attribute the thought to another agent. How could a person come to have the impression that, although she is the subject in whom a certain thought occurs, she does not *think* the thought? What may explain her experience of externality? The following hypothesis suggests itself:

First externality hypothesis   A person denies that she is the agent of a given thought because she discovers that she cannot voluntarily control its occurrence in her. The thought seems to come unbidden and she cannot dismiss it at will or prevent its recurrence.

Certainly, subjects who suffer from voices or inserted thoughts generally feel as if the alien thought or inner speech forces itself upon them. Although they may learn to banish the thought by holding their mouths open, or by some other distracting maneuver, they do not enjoy the direct, voluntary control over it that they exercise over their "normal" thoughts. However, attention to another sort of disturbance of one's sense of voluntary control over one's thoughts shows that this first externality hypothesis is problematic.

People who suffer from obsessive compulsive thought disorder have the powerful impression that they are at the mercy of their obsessional thoughts and find themselves unable to control their occurrence. Nevertheless, as we noted in our discussion of Hoffman, such people typically experience these thoughts as their own. For example, Fish (1985, p. 43) contrasts obsessional thinking with the experience of thought insertion:

While the obsessional patient recognizes that he is compelled to think about things against his will, he does not regard the thoughts as foreign, i.e., he recognizes that they are his own thoughts.

Sims (1995, p. 307) also emphasizes that patients experience obsessive thoughts as their own. Rapaport (1989, p. 139) notes that some obsessives entertain the possibility that their obsessive thoughts are not their own, but she remarks that this is not common and that full-blown delusions of thought insertion are rare. Hoffman (1986, p. 536) likewise denies that obsessives experience their thoughts as "unintended," in contrast to the hallucinators' experience of voices.

It seems that subjects entertaining compulsive thoughts generally do regard the thoughts as agentically their own, despite their sense of lack of normal, voluntary control over the thoughts in question. Thus, it does not seem advisable to identify the sense of agency with the sense of voluntary control over thought.

Another sort of hypothesis, suggested by Louis Sass, looks more promising. Like Hoffman and Frith, Sass (1992, p. 214) supposes that we generally have a sense of active involvement in our inner lives: "Normally one does have the sense of living one's perceptions, thoughts, and actions as if from within, with an implicit or semiconscious sense of intention and control." Sass connects this sense of living one's mental life from within with the idea that one normally experiences a sort of self-organizing unity among one's perceptions, thoughts, and actions. One sees oneself as an "integrated motivational and cognitive universe, a dynamic center of awareness, emotion, judgment, and action organized into a distinctive whole" (p. 215). (Here Sass is quoting Geertz 1983.) One's sense that one's thoughts and actions are one's own depends on one's ability to locate them within this integrated personal universe. However, in the self-disturbances associated with schizophrenia—among which Sass numbers both verbal hallucinations and thought insertion—the experienced unity of self breaks down. A person finds that he cannot organize his emotions, thoughts, and actions into an integrated personal whole. Particular thoughts and actions may seem not to "make sense" in relation to the whole. As a result, the subject "may lose the feeling that his thoughts belong to him" (Sass 1992, p. 214). He may "feel that his sensations and thoughts originate somehow outside his own . . . mind" (ibid., p. 228).

Sass explains this loss of the sense of unity of the self as a by-product of "relentless introspection." In his view, maintaining the sense of unity requires a certain inattention to the processes and elements of inner life. Look too close and you lose your grip on the big picture. Unable to be content with a global impression of unity, the schizophrenic subject scrutinizes his mental universe, searching out the joints between its various components. "Rather than sustaining a sense of self," this "hyperreflexive" observation "may actually serve to undermine it" (ibid., p. 230).

We shall not further explore Sass's account of how the person loses her sense of the unity of the self. However, we do want to follow up on his tempting suggestion that the subject's sense of agency regarding episodes in her psychological history might depend on her ability to integrate them into her larger picture of herself. This suggestion meshes well with a view, propounded by Dennett (1981, 1987, 1991) and Flanagan (1991, 1992), that connects our sense that we lead or author our lives with our proclivity to construct self-referential descriptions and explanations that organize the episodes in our lives into coherent projectable patterns. One of our favorite self-referential explanatory strategies as persons, and the source which we propose for our susceptibility to experiences of alienation, is to explain particular episodes of behavior or occurrent mental episodes as expressions of our underlying, relatively more persistent intentional states, such as our beliefs and desires. We adopt what Dennett calls the "intentional stance" toward ourselves. Our self-referential intentional explanations make sense of our activities and provide the basis for predictions of or expectations about our future behavior. Collectively they constitute a kind of theory (or, more loosely, conception) of our own agency or intentional psychology. In the words of Flanagan (1992, p. 196), they are "the story that we tell ourselves to understand ourselves for who we are."

In the spirit of Sass, Dennett, and Flanagan, we propose the following hypothesis:

Second externality hypothesis A person denies that she is the agent of a given thought because she finds that she cannot explain its occurrence in terms of her theory or conception of her intentional psychology.

As an aid to explaining this hypothesis, let us consider a hypothetical example of a clinical sort: Bruce, a patient in a state psychiatric hospital, is tiptoeing up to the ward dinner trolley holding a bottle of urine in his hand. He is moving in this fashion because he believes that, if he attracts the attention of the orderly, the orderly will prevent him from reaching the trolley; he wants to reach the trolley; and he believes that tiptoeing is the surest way to move without attracting the orderly's attention. Bruce anticipates that, on reaching the trolley, he will upend the bottle of urine over the trolley, because he wants to demonstrate his contempt for the charlatans who have unjustly confined him in this asylum, he believes that covering the trolley with his urine is the best way of demonstrating his contempt, and he believes that the easiest way to get the urine from the bottle onto the trolley is to upend the bottle over the trolley. Bruce's activity seems sensible or intelligible to him because he takes it to be an expression of his beliefs and desires. He therefore experiences it as something he is doing, as his action, and he regards himself as its agent.

Taking an activity to be an expression of one's own beliefs and desires may occur for a variety of reasons. On some theoretical accounts, the person is said to consciously experience, perhaps even to immediately feel, a causal connection between his intentions to act and the bodily activities that result from those intentions (Wakefield and Dreyfus 1993). The experience of acting contains within it the experience of the motion's or action's being caused and directed by the intention. On this theoretical conception, Bruce's experience of causality between the intention to upend the bottle and the upending tells him that the upending is *his* action. He feels himself intentionally upending the bottle.

As may be expected from our remarks earlier in the book on the introspectability of propositional attitudes, we are not attracted to the unabashedly introspectionist notion that we introspect or feel causal connections between our intentions and actions. However, there is a quasi-introspectionist alternative to this idea which, we believe, is appealing and explanatorily fruitful. This is that persons may sense or perceive the moment-by-moment appropriateness or suitability of their actions to their perceived circumstances, or their sense of what they are like or about, and therein spontaneously surmise from this sensed suitability that they possess and are acting upon intentions which are responsible for the action. In such a manner, an action may impress a person as his own. Bruce's activity may strike him as sensible or suitable in his circumstances. It therein impresses him as brought about by himself.

In Bruce's and similar cases, a person may not consciously represent or deliberate about his intentions before he acts (though he may). He may act with little or no deliberation or forethought. He may even be startled or surprised when the action is performed, although he still attributes it to himself. "I did that? Well, I did." Moreover these unthinking activities may strike persons as typical or characteristic of themselves, perhaps in their manner or content, given their conception of themselves. The actions may conform to their "theory" of what they are like and thus likely to do as persons. Consider in this connection the following remark by the former basketball star Larry Bird, in which he describes the complex motion of passing a ball during a game:

[A lot of things] I do on the court are just reactions to situations. . . . I don't think about some of the things that I am trying to do. . . . A lot of times I've passed the basketball and not realized I've passed it until a moment or so later. (quoted in Wakefield and Dreyfus 1993, p. 265; originally in Levine 1988)

Bird's passing behavior includes perceiving its fitness or appropriateness to his situation and experiencing it as just the sort of thing that he characteristically does. This sense of fit to circumstance and of stemming from himself does not mean that Bird literally feels the actual *causing* of his action by his intention to pass, but it helps to explain why he experiences the action as his own. He supposes that an intention to pass was his and therefore that the behavior of passing was his.

Bruce, of course, is no Larry Bird. Suppose, in a second hypothetical scenario for Bruce, that he finds himself unable to account for his ambulatory behavior, given his beliefs about his intentional states. He has no conception of why he is walking on tiptoe or carrying the bottle of urine. The whole thing seems inappropriate in his circumstances. He cannot guess when he will stop walking or what may happen when he does. He does not take himself to have any beliefs or desires that would "rationalize" or "suit" his behavior to circumstance, nor do any of his beliefs about his current intentional states give him any basis for predicting what will happen next. In such a case as this, his behavior will not appear to him as *his* action. It will not seem to him that *he* personally is involved in what is happening to him.

Bruce then has two—at least two—interpretative options: (1) He may revise his understanding of his own intentional psychology and of the appropriateness of his behavior so as to infer that he does possess or harbor intentional states suitably expressed by his current behavior; he therein believes that the behavior is his action. (2) He may determine that what is going on is none of his doing—perhaps he is possessed—and that he is involved in these events only as patient and not as agent.

We propose that a person's sense that he is the thinker or agent of his *mental* activity—of his conscious thoughts and feelings—likewise depends on his conviction that his occurrent mental episodes express his intentional states. That is, whether a person regards a thought (subjectively) in him as something that he *thinks*, rather than as a mere episode in his psychological history, depends upon whether he finds it explicable in terms of his conception of what he believes and desires. For thinking, as for overt behavior, your awareness that you are *doing* something requires having a sense of what you are doing and why you are doing it. It requires a sense of the personal circumstances of the action.

Suppose that, like Bruce, I find the thought "I must empty the urine bottle over the trolley" occurring in me. Or suppose that, like Larry Bird, I think "Pass now." Do I regard this as something that I think, as my own impulse, or do I dismiss it as a piece of random mentation or stray verbal imagery? The answer will depend on whether I take myself to have beliefs and desires and other intentional states of the sort that would rationalize its occurrence in me and make these appropriate thoughts for me. If my self-referential explanation of my own mental activity attributes to me a relevant set of intentional states, I may unproblematically accept the impulse as my own mentation, something internal to me in the agentically self-attributive sense. If not, then I must either revise my self-understanding or conclude that

the episode is not my doing but represents something external to
me.

Why might I fail to embrace an intentional, agentic explanation of a thought I find occurring in me? Why do "alien"
thoughts seem "unsuitable"? As Hoffman (1986, p. 515) notes, the
"traditional psychoanalytic" account of voices assumes that
the voice expresses ideas that are unacceptable or distasteful to the
person and that he therefore disavows or dissociates from them.
Perhaps, then, I fail to find an explanation of the relevant thoughts
within my theory or conception of my intentional psychology—
my self-referential narrative—because I don't want to find such
an explanation.

Frankfurt (1988) supposes that a person's evaluative attitudes
toward a mental episode play a crucial role in determining
whether that episode is experienced as internal or external to the
person. Why should a person regard an episode in his psychological history as external? "The answer that comes most readily
to mind," Frankfurt writes (p. 63), "is that passions are external to
us just when we prefer not to have them . . . and that they are
internal when, at the time of their occurrence, we welcome or
indifferently accept them. On this account a passion is uniquely
ours when it is what we want to feel, or are willing to feel, while
a passion whose occurrence in us we disapprove is not strictly
ours."

Why should we prefer not to have a certain passion or
other conscious episode occur in us? Because, Frankfurt says
(p. 163), "we care about what we are. We are ceaselessly alert to
the danger that there may be discrepancies between what we wish
to be . . . and how we actually appear to others and to ourselves."
Personal self-attribution here reveals a strong evaluative component. I may find in my stream of consciousness elements such

that, were I to acknowledge them as "strictly" or "personally" my own, I would be forced to admit that I am not the sort of person I wish and perhaps believe myself to be. Externalizing such elements allows me to preserve my self-image or self-esteem—what Frankfurt (p. 63) calls "our preferred conception of ourselves."

This evaluative attitude-based hypothesis closely parallels explanations of experiences of alienation common in the clinical literature. Freud (1959, p. 156) suggests that patients attribute their own thoughts to others in order to preserve "internalized standards of good and bad." Eagle (1988, pp. 92, 98) speaks of mental episodes' being "purposively disowned" because they are "sharply at variance with my sense of . . . what I want to think." Snyder (1974, p. 121) explains that verbal hallucinations allow the subject to "no longer take responsibility" for mental processes that the subject finds "unbearable." The attribution to alters (nonselves) in multiple personality disorder often is described as a coping mechanism to avoid unwelcome recollections of childhood abuse (Braude 1995; Gillett 1986, 1991; Hacking 1995).

However, it is obvious that not all thoughts found to be distasteful or threatening to self-esteem are experienced as voices or as alien insertions or even as agentically external. Frankfurt acknowledges that a person may accept a thought as something he *thinks*, "even when he regrets this fact and wishes that [the thought] did not occur in him." He writes of the person becoming "resigned to being someone of whom he himself does not altogether approve" (p. 64).

Even thoughts that cause the subject great distress may be accepted by her as expressions of her own agency. Consider again the subject's attitudes toward her obsessive thoughts. As we previously noted, subjects suffering from obsessive compulsive thought disorder typically regard the thoughts as their own.

Nevertheless, as Fish (1985, p. 37) observes, "one of the most important features of obsessions is that their content is of such a nature as to cause the sufferer great anxiety and guilt. [They] are particularly repugnant to the individual: the prudish person is tormented by sexual thoughts, the religious person by blasphemous thoughts." If persons do not experience their obsessive thoughts to be their own, agentically, if, for example, they attribute the thoughts to themselves only in the subjective sense, they should, presumably, not feel guilty about entertaining such thoughts.

Although in his account of externalization, Frankfurt allows that a negative evaluation of an episode does not suffice to explain its externality or nonself attribution, he does suggest that a person's disapproval is a necessary condition:

The fact that a person disapproves of a passion is . . . not a sufficient condition of the passion's externality to him. On the other hand, it may be that disapproval is a necessary condition of externality. It is in fact difficult to think of a convincing example in which a person to whom a passion is external nonetheless approves of the occurrence of the passion in him. [This] supports the conjecture that a person's approval of a passion that occurs in his history is a sufficient condition of the passion's being internal to him. (p. 65)

However, clinical reports of voices and thought insertion do not support the notion that disapproval is a necessary condition for experiences of alienation. Contents of inserted thoughts and of voices are by no means invariably threatening or distressing. For example, Bleuler's classic study of schizophrenia says of verbal hallucinations that "the usual occurrence is that the "voices" threaten, curse, criticize, and console in short sentences or abrupt words" (1950, p. 96). While noting that "threats and curses form the main and most common content of those voices," Bleuler remarks that "besides their persecutors the patients often hear the voice of some protector" (ibid.). Snyder (1974, p. 119) observes that "in the most common type of hallucination, the voices threaten or condemn the patient, or almost as frequently console him." Modell (1960) takes special pains to emphasize that voices are quite often innocuous, offering instructions or advice. These observations are supported by Mott, Small, and Anderson (1965) and by Linn (1977). Taylor and Heiser (1971) make the same sorts of point about inserted thoughts.

Voices in nonpsychotics have been extensively studied by Foulkes and his collaborators. (See, e.g., Foulkes and Scott 1965.) Distressing or accusatory voices are said to be quite uncommon in such cases. A particularly interesting study by Hamilton (1985) reports that athetoid-spastic quadriplegics, who are quite prone to verbal hallucinations, almost invariably find their "voices" comforting and reassuring.

The cases recounted above show that a person may regard an episode as agentically alien although he does not disapprove of its occurrence. Of course, he may feel indulgent toward the relevant episode only so long as he regards it as not his own. Perhaps his "ideal image" of himself would be threatened were he to acknowledge active involvement in the episode. Perhaps he does not mind being the sort of subject in whose psychological history a salacious thought may occur, but his self-esteem would be threatened by acknowledging himself to be the sort of *person* who would *think* such a thought. However, the contents of alienated thoughts often are emotionally neutral or reassuring. Chapman and Chapman (1998) report the case of a young woman who persistently heard the voices of her father and her paternal grandmother, both deceased, advising her on various decisions that she faced, such as whether to buy a car. She regarded their intervention as well-intentioned and actually helpful to her. There seems no obvious reason why this patient's self-esteem would be threatened should she acknowledge that she is the sort of person who would weigh the pros and cons of purchasing an automobile.

Of course, one can tell other stories about what motivates a person to disown his or her alien thoughts. Our account of attribution of mental agency—the second externality hypothesis above—can readily accommodate motivational factors. We need only suppose that a subject's tendency to entertain or accept intentional explanations of particular thoughts may be biased or primed by evaluative attitudes toward those thoughts. Should a blasphemous thought occur in her, for example, an individual's preference for maintaining an image of herself as a pious person might make her less likely to accept, or even unable to entertain, the hypothesis that she harbors the sorts of beliefs and desires that would find their natural expression in blasphemous thoughts. She would feel that such thoughts could not occur by her own doing.

However, we do not see any reason to believe that a person's failure to accept agentic responsibility for a thought *must* be explained in motivational terms. What our account of the sense of mental agency presupposes is that the subject will not accept as agentically her own thoughts whose occurrence she finds inexplicable by reference to her conception or self-referential description of her intentional states. We do not commit ourselves to any motivational story of why she finds them inexplicable. Indeed, perhaps on some occasions a person fails to find an intentional explanation for a given thought because there isn't one. Thoughts may occur in her that do not express, or do not express suitably, any of her underlying intentional states.

This is, of course, what Hoffman proposes in his account of the causal mechanics of verbal hallucinations. Breakdowns of the processes that normally guide the production of inner speech result in episodes of inner speech that are not consonant with the subject's intentions.

Whatever one's view of Hoffman's detailed account, his assumption that a thought occurring in my mind might fail to impress me as expressive of my underlying beliefs and desires is quite plausible. When a person feels that some of her thoughts are not her own doing, her impression might be correct.

Even if my alien thoughts are due to my own agency, my failure to recognize this fact need not represent motivated self-deception. A Frithian lapse of monitoring or a Sassian bout of relentless introspection might impair my ability to appreciate the intentional origins of my thoughts. Perhaps I am some sort of super-rationalist who always does intend to think whatever thoughts occur in me. That doesn't ensure that I always *recognize* that I have the relevant intentions, or that my failure to accept agentic responsibility must arise from my unwillingness to face the truth about myself.

Not only do we reject the idea that the failure to recognize relevant intentions must be explained in motivational terms; we don't see why there must be a single explanation of any sort that covers all cases. It may be necessary to tell different stories about why the subject finds her thoughts intentionally inexplicable in various cases. Perhaps her self-referential narrative or conception of her underlying intentional states is fragmented, indeterminate, or difficult to apply in certain situations. What thoughts stem from her is not "transparent" to her. Her Sassian overarching sense of herself—of her own personal universe—is epistemically elusive or under construction and lacks the kind of explanatory homogeneity and projectability possessed by other people's mental universes.[1]

8.3   Explaining Alienation

From what does the experience of alienation arise? A person who experiences delusions of thought insertion does more than deny that she is the agent behind her thoughts; she maintains that another thinks in her. Why should she experience her thoughts as *alien*, as expressions of another's mental agency rather than as mere mental happenings?

Our proposed explanation for the extraordinary hypothesis of alienation is derived from our second externality hypothesis for experiences of nonself attribution. It goes as follows: Despite a person's conviction that an episode of thinking does not express her underlying psychology (and, thus, is not agentically her own), the episode may still impress her as intentional. Unlike nonvoluntary mental activity, such as snatches of doggerel running through one's head (which are notable for their lack of fit with and their tendency to distract a person from her current concerns or situation), the contents of alien thoughts tend to be intelligently structured and even personally salient to their subjects (Bleuler 1950, p. 97; Mott, Small, and Anderson 1965). They mean something to the person; they seem like actions even if they don't seem like her own actions. Similarly, in the case of voices, alien verbal imagery typically possesses the sorts of grammatical forms that are appropriate for conversational or communicative speech. For example, often they are in the second person (Linn 1977).

1. Recall Marilyn Monroe's observation about her struggle with self-comprehension (note 1 to chapter 5).

Often they are in an imperative mood (Bleuler 1950). Their content is similar to communicative acts like giving advice or criticism, issuing threats and orders, offering condolence or encouragement.

A recent paper (Hoffman et al. 1994, p. 1230) asserts that "hallucinated voices demonstrate recurrent subject-specific semantic content that was pronounced as normal conversational discourse," and that "it is plausible, therefore, that schizophrenia patients infer that their hallucinated voices derive from a particular source or speaker capable of language productions that are at least as organized . . . as those of an ordinary speaker."

Suppose that Mary, a young mother concerned with her child's welfare and her own maternal responsibilities, finds the thought "Bad mother," or "You're hurting your child," or "Joan Crawford!" occurring in her stream of consciousness. She does not acknowledge in herself or attribute to herself the sorts of intentional states that would naturally find expression in these thoughts. She pictures herself as a caring, competent mother, utterly devoted to her child; so these are not the sorts of comments she would make or wish to make to herself. They also don't seem to fit her circumstance (for instance, her child is not misbehaving). They strike her as contextually unsuitable and personally uncharacteristic. Nonetheless, it is hard for her to dismiss these thoughts as random mental activities. They seem to betray an agency, an intelligence, that accounts for their coherence, salience, and directedness. Thus, she may have the strong impression that *someone* is thinking in, or speaking to her.

Whether Mary's experience of alienation becomes a full-blown delusional conviction depends, no doubt, on a variety of factors—cultural, psychosocial, and neurological—that go beyond immediate phenomenology. However, as far as the experience itself is concerned, our hypothesis is that the apparent intelligence of the thoughts provides the experiential or epistemic basis for attributing them to another agent. Mary experiences her thoughts as "personal" (intelligently composed by someone), but not as expressive of her own person.

Another example involving overt behavior may be helpful here: Suppose I find myself taking up a pen and rapidly inscribing marks on a piece of paper. To my surprise, I discover that these marks form English words and sentences—words and sentences that would naturally be used to express undying love for someone named Beatrice. My movements with the pen seem to be producing a letter. Such literary production suggests authorial direction. However, I am not aware of providing that direction. I recollect no one named Beatrice. I do not seem to myself to have any beliefs and desires that such a letter would appropriately express. I have no idea which sentence will appear next on the page or when the letter will end. Still, it hardly seems possible to me that there is no intelligent agent behind my performance.

Provided I remain convinced that composing the letter is an intelligent performance, an action or activity, I have two options. One is to suppose that the writing is after all something that I am doing. I revise my conception of myself so as to accommodate in my psychology the sorts of intentional states required for the performance: "I do after all know a Beatrice." "I do after all want to express my love to her." "I am after all the author of this letter." Perhaps I will supplement this revision with some explanation of why I was previously unaware of these intentional states: "Beatrice is my neighbor's wife." "I dread to admit that I covet my neighbor's wife." The second option is to suppose that someone else is using me to write a love letter to Beatrice. He is writing the letter through me or through my body. I conclude that I am possessed, that my movements are directed by the intentional states of another and express his beliefs and desires.

Now imagine, by analogy, that, instead of finding myself taking up a pen and writing to Beatrice, I find myself thinking of such a person and entertaining verbal imagery of love of her. Similarly, the movements of my conscious mind, my thoughts or inner speech, may seem to me to be intelligent but not to express my own intelligence; they don't fit anything I am doing at the time. Instead they seem to be manifestations of another person. Attribution to another would certainly be an extraordinary hypothesis in the case of writing to Beatrice, and an extra-extraordinary hypothesis regarding the provenance of these thoughts about Beatrice. However, the highly atypical character of my current thoughts, combined perhaps with my imperative emotional needs may lead me to embrace it.

What we are claiming about thought insertion and voices by treating them as more or less similar phenomena for explanatory purposes is close to various of Hoffman's, Frith's, and Frankfurt's remarks on alienation and externality. Our tale is Hoffmanian insofar as we assume that the experience of externality can be epistemically warranted (subjectively if not *tout court*) given certain introspective evidence about the failure to concord with one's intentions or underlying attitudes. The tale is Frithian in its allegiance to a unified explanation of both voices and delusions of thought insertion. The mere fact that some voices have audible quality does not mean that voices in general must be explained differently from cases of thought insertion. The story is Frankfurtian insofar as it assumes that people experience themselves in action, as agents behind their own activities, whether the action is bodily or mental. We may be conscious of ourselves as arm raisers and not merely as subjects with rising arms. We may experience ourselves as thinkers and not merely as subjects in whom thoughts occur.

8.4   Concluding Compulsively

What we are outlining here is a schematic and speculative account of the experience of alienation, as distinguished from a detailed and clinically confirmed account. We will not belabor the point, but we know of no detailed and confirmed account. If we did, we would adopt it. We have helped ourselves to speculation in hopes that it contributes to *some* progress in the understanding of alienation. The centerpiece of our understanding is the notion that thought insertion and nonauditory voices represent the coming apart of two strands in self-conscious experience: the senses of subjectivity and agency.

In this concluding section, we shall briefly consider how thought insertion and nonauditory verbal hallucinations relate to two other disturbances of one's sense of one's thoughts: obsessive compulsive thinking and delusions of alien influence. Finally, we shall consider how voices and inserted thoughts relate to each other.

The crucial difference between experiences of voices or inserted thoughts, on the one hand, and compulsive thinking, on the other hand, is that the subject regards the former as alien, as attributable to another, while the subject experiences compulsive thoughts as her own. However, in both sorts of cases the subject experiences her thoughts as somehow not under her intentional control. This led Junginger (1986) to suppose that in both cases the subject experiences the relevant thoughts as unintended by her. He then challenged Hoffman to explain why compulsive thoughts are not also experienced as alien, since, on Hoffman's view, (merely) experiencing verbal imagery as unintended leads the subject, "more or less automatically," to infer that the imagery is of alien origin (Hoffman 1986, p. 126).

As will be recalled, merely experiencing thoughts as unintended does not lead subjects automatically to the impression that they are expressions of another's agency. However, we do wish to claim that, if the subject experiences a thought as unintended by her, she will deny that it is an expression of her own agency—that is, that she *thinks* the thought. Thus, it might seem that, on our own account, subjects should deny that they *think* their compulsive thoughts. Obsessive compulsive thinkers should deny, to use our terms, that their thoughts are agentically their own. In such a case, we would be forced to interpret the clinical observation that obsessive thinkers recognize their thoughts as their own as an indication that the subjects recognize them as their own in the merely subjective sense: as episodes in their psychological history.

We certainly believe that there are cases where subjects experience episodes in their mental lives as not agentically their own without experiencing them as agentically alien (that is, as occurring in them through someone else's agency). However, we resist the suggestion that obsessive compulsive thought disorder is best understood in such terms. Rather, we want to claim, with Hoffman, that the obsessive compulsive thinker experiences her thoughts as intended by her, as agentically her own. Hoffman (1986, p. 536) replies to Junginger as follows:

Although it is true that obsessional thoughts cannot be controlled, obsessional thoughts . . . are not unintended in the sense in which I have defined the term. Obsessives generally have ready conscious access to the goal of their obsessive compulsiveness.

Or, as we would prefer to put it, obsessives do take themselves to have beliefs and desires of the sort that explain their obsessive thoughts. For example, the obsessive who finds the thought "I may have left the door unlocked; I'd better check it again" occurring in her does suppose that she doubts whether she locked the door and that she desires to be sure that the door is locked. These intentional states do rationalize and make sense to her of her thought, as far as she is concerned. Thus, she has the sense that "I may have left the door unlocked; I'd better check it" is something that she *thinks*.

Of course, the obsessive in question may regard the putative intentional states as imprudent or unhealthy. She has checked the lock three times, and she cannot understand why this hasn't put her doubts to rest. She doesn't believe it to be all that important whether the door is locked, and she puzzles over why she should so strongly desire to ensure that it is. She may wish that she could free herself from these doubts and desires, or at least she may resist the impulse to express them in thought and action. However, she seems unable to resist, and thus she feels compelled, as Fish (1985, p. 43) puts it, "to think about things against her will." But, she experiences these thoughts as things she *thinks*, not merely as things that happen in her psychological history.

Because the above Hoffmanian account does a superior job of capturing the standard clinical distinction between thought insertion and compulsive thought disorder, we favor it over the proposal that obsessive thoughts are experienced as unintended. As we noted, obsessives tend to feel responsible for their obsessive thoughts: to feel that they ought not think them. If the subject regarded these thoughts as mere happenings, as none of her doing, their occurrence might annoy or distress her, but it would not make her feel blameworthy.

What about delusions of influence? Regarding delusions of influence, we noted above that the clinical literature distinguishes the subject's having the impression that another influences or controls her thinking from the experience of alienation in thought insertion. To quote again from Fulford (1989, p. 221):

The experience of one's own thoughts being influenced is like thought insertion to the extent that it is something that is "done or happens" to one . . . [but] that which is being done is simply the *influencing* of one's thoughts; whereas in the case of thought insertion it is (bizarrely) the thinking itself.

Or, as Wing (1988, p. 105) expresses it, the subject experiencing thought insertion supposes, not that another has caused her to have certain thoughts, "but that the thoughts themselves are not" hers. Recall also that we criticized Frith's account of thought insertion because it fails to explain the distinction between thought insertion and experiences of alien influence or control.

This raises the question of how we wish to distinguish thought insertion from experiences of influence. After all, in both cases the subject has the impression that someone else has caused a thought to occur in her mind. In both cases she feels that the relevant thoughts express another's agency. What's the difference?

We propose that the difference between the subject's experience of her thoughts in the two cases lies in *how* she represents the other as causing the relevant thoughts to occur in her mind. The merely influenced subject believes that the other has caused *her* to think the thought—i.e., that the other agent has caused her to have the underlying intentional states that cause her to think the thought. The other exerts his influence *through* her agency— he manipulates her agency. In thought insertion, by contrast, the subject believes that the other actually has done the thinking for her. She has not been manipulated into thinking something.

Instead, her agency or intentional economy has been bypassed entirely. She denies having any of the intentions that find expression in the occurrence of the thought. She supposes that these intentions lie outside her ego boundary, in the other.

To appreciate the difference between these two ways of viewing the occurrence of a thought, compare the following two ways in which another can cause my arm to go up: (1) He can cause me to raise my arm myself; for example, he might psychologically influence me so that I perform the action of raising my arm by causing me to want to raise my arm, or to believe that I need to raise it for some reason. (2) He can raise my arm for me, by grasping it and picking it up or by electrically stimulating my deltoid muscles. In (1), raising my arm is something that the other causes *me* to do; in (2), raising my arm is the other person's action and not something that I do.

The above comparison provides a conceptual means of distinguishing experiences of influence from experiences of thought insertion. It does not pretend to explain why a particular person would conceive of his or her situation in one way or the other. We propose that victims of influence suppose themselves to harbor, perhaps in some sense against their will, the intentional states expressed in their thoughts. Victims of thought insertion do not embrace this supposition. However, we offer no hypothesis concerning why a particular subject might embrace or fail to embrace this supposition.

What, if anything, distinguishes thought insertion from nonauditory voices? We have proposed that the experience of alienation works the same way in both cases. That is, in each case the subject regards an episode in her mental life as alien, in the sense that its occurrence in her expresses someone else's agency: it is the other's action rather than her own. But this does not entail that the *overall* experience is the same in thought insertion and in nonauditory verbal hallucinations. There is a presumptive reason to believe that the overall experience differs in these two cases: Patients offer different descriptions. "Someone is inserting his thoughts into my mind" differs from "I was aware of another's voice, which I did not perceive with my senses, but felt within my mind." However, these might simply be different ways of trying to capture or communicate the same experience. That a person chooses to express herself in one way rather than the other might reflect factors independent of the experience. Her particular life history, or her cultural or educational background, might make one description more available to her or more appropriate for her than the other.

Some philosophers deny that there is any fact of the psychological matter about whether, in talking about different experiences, we are dealing with different experiences or merely with different descriptions of the same experience. But before we throw up our hands and pronounce the question moot it would be useful to know whether further inquiry would uncover some systematic variations in patients' reports of thought insertion and voices. One theoretical possibility is that subjects of inserted thoughts might report that the alien thoughts seem to be smoothly integrated into their stream of consciousness, and that they become suspicious of them by reflecting upon their content. This content may seem personally anomalous or uncharacteristic in light of their conception of themselves. Voices, by contrast, might be described as breaking in on the stream of consciousness, taking the subject by surprise and in a manner similar to being taken by surprise by the interruption of another's voice. Voices may grab attention by the way in which they occur as much as, or perhaps even more than, by what they actually say.

Perhaps experiencing inserted thoughts is more like finding that you lapsed into a daydream or fantasy without meaning to, or without even really noticing when your thoughts slipped into another track. "Hearing" a voice, by contrast, might seem more like having your thinking interrupted when someone unexpectedly addresses you.

We stress that the above possibilities are purely hypothetical. We do not know what results may appear if people who report voices or inserted thoughts are encouraged to say more about their experiences. It is worth noting, however, that attention to the exact ways in which patients describe their experiences and systematic attempts to get them to elaborate and reflect on their spontaneous reports are what led clinicians to recognize that not all the episodes classified as verbal hallucinations are auditory or audition-like experiences. (See Junginger and Frame 1985.)

It might be particularly revealing to talk to subjects who report both voices and inserted thoughts. Statistics on the frequency with which various symptoms occur in patients diagnosed as schizophrenic suggest that there must be a number of such patients. In one such study (Sartorius et al. 1977), 70 percent of such patients experienced verbal hallucinations, while 52 percent experienced thought insertion. This indicates that there must have been substantial overlap. What would these patients say if asked how they tell the difference between voices and inserted thoughts? We don't have an answer to this question. We have found no indication in the clinical literature that it has ever been asked. Thus, in the end, we have no view about how nonauditory voices might be distinguished from inserted thoughts. We maintain that they present us with a similar conceptual puzzle: How can a person acknowledge that a thought or voice occurs in her mind while denying that it is her thought or voice? We also claim that in both cases the conceptual puzzle can be resolved in the same manner, namely by deploying the distinction between the sense of subjectivity and the sense of agency. Finally, we claim that the sense of agency operative in both inserted thoughts and voices is constituted by our self-referential narratives or conceptions of our underlying intentional states.

It would be premature, of course, to conclude that we are on the verge of an all-out understanding of human self-experience and of alienated self-consciousness. The sense of subjectivity/sense of agency distinction is conceptually and clinically uncharted territory, and we have little knowledge of what theoretical and experimental possibilities and dangers lurk within the distinction and within its application to breakdowns of self-consciousness. A humbling voice warns us: "There is a lot left to learn."

Bibliography

Akins, K. A., and Dennett, D. C. 1986. Who may I say is calling? *Behavioral and Brain Sciences* 9: 517–518.

Allen, J. F., Halpern, J., and Friend, R. 1985. Removal and diversion tactics and the control of auditory hallucinations. *Behavior Research and Therapy* 23: 601–605.

Alpert, M. 1986. Language production process and hallucination phenomenology. *Behavioral and Brain Sciences* 9: 518–519.

Alpert, M., and Silvers, J. 1970. Perceptual characteristics distinguishing auditory hallucinations in schizophrenia and acute alcoholic psychoses. *American Journal of Psychiatry* 127: 298–302.

American Psychiatric Association. 1994. *Diagnostic and Statistical Manual of Mental Disorders*, fourth edition. American Psychiatric Association.

Ames, D. 1984. Self-shooting of a phantom head. *British Journal of Psychiatry* 145: 193–194.

Arieti, S. 1967. *The Intrapsychic Self*. Basic Books.

Armstrong, D. M. 1968. *A Materialist Theory of Mind*. Routledge and Kegan Paul.

Baddeley, A. 1986. *Working Memory*. Oxford University Press.

Baillarger, J. 1846. *Des Hallucinations*. Bailliere.

Bechtel, W., Abrahamsen, A., and Graham, G. 1998. The life of cognitive science. In *A Companion to Cognitive Science*, ed. W. Bechtel and G. Graham.

Bechtel, W., and Richardson, R. C. 1993. *Discovering Complexity: Decomposition and Localization as Strategies*. Princeton University Press.

Bentall, R. P., and Slade, P. D. 1985. Reality testing and auditory hallucinations: a signal detection analysis. *British Journal of Clinical Psychology* 24: 159–169.

Bick, P. A., and Kinsbourne, M. 1987. Auditory hallucinations and subvocal speech in schizophrenic patients. *American Journal of Psychiatry* 4: 222–225.

Bleuler, E. 1934. *Textbook of Psychiatry*, trans. A. A. Brill. Macmillan.

Bleuler, E. 1950. *Dementia Praecox or the Group of Schizophrenias*. International University Press.

Bliss, E. 1986. *Multiple Personality, Allied Disorders, and Hypnosis*. Oxford University Press.

Block, N. 1993. Review of D. C. Dennett's *Consciousness Explained*, *Journal of Philosophy* 90: 181–193.

Braude, S. 1995. *First Person Plural: Multiple Personality and the Philosophy of Mind*. Rowman and Littlefield.

Chapman, J. 1966. Early symptoms of schizophrenia. *British Journal of Psychiatry* 12: 225–251.

Chapman, L. J., and Chapman, J. P. 1988. The genesis of delusions. In *Delusional Beliefs*, ed. T. Oltmanns and B. Maher. Wiley.

Chisholm, R. 1976. *Person and Object: A Metaphysical Study*. Open Court.

Chisholm, R. 1981. *The First Person: An Essay on Reference and Intentionality*. University of Minnesota.

Churchland, P. S. 1983. Consciousness: the transmutation of a concept. *Pacific Philosophical Quarterly* 64: 80–95.

Coleman, M., and Gillborg, C. 1996. *A Biological Approach to the Schizophrenic Spectrum of Disorders*. Springer.

Confer, W. N., and Ables, B. S. 1983. *Multiple Personality: Etiology, Diagnosis, and Treatment*. Human Sciences Press.

Critchley, E. M. R., Denmark, J. C., Warren, F., and Wilson, K. A. 1981. Hallucinatory experiences in prelingually profoundly deaf schizophrenics. *British Journal of Psychiatry* 138: 30–32.

Cutting, J. 1995. Descriptive psychopathology. In *Schizophrenia*, ed. S. Hirsch and D. Weinberger. Blackwell.

Dennett, D. C. 1981. *Brainstorms*. MIT Press.

Dennett, D. C. 1987. *The Intentional Stance*. MIT Press.

Dennett, D. C. 1991. *Consciousness Explained*. Little, Brown.

Eagle, M. 1988. Psychoanalysis and the person. In *Mind, Psychoanalysis, and Science*, ed. P. Clark and C. Wright. Blackwell.

Fish, F. J. 1962. *Fish's Schizophrenia*, third edition, ed. M. Hamilton. Wright, 1984.

Fish, F. J. 1985. *Clinical Psychopathology: Signs and Symptoms in Psychiatry*, ed. M. Hamilton. Wright.

Flanagan, O. 1991. *Varieties of Moral Personality: Ethics and Psychological Realism*. Harvard University Press.

Flanagan, O. 1992. *Consciousness Reconsidered*. MIT Press.

Flanagan, O. 1994. Multiple identity, character transformation, and self-reclamation. In *Philosophical Psychopathology*, ed. G. Graham and G. Stephens. MIT Press.

Flor-Henry, P. 1986. Auditory hallucinations, inner speech, and the dominant hemisphere. *Behavioral and Brain Sciences* 9: 523–524.

Foulkes, D., and Fleisher, S. 1975. Mental activity in relaxed wakefulness. *Journal of Abnormal Psychology* 84: 66–75.

Foulkes, D., and Scott, E. 1973. An above-zero waking baseline for the incidence of momentarily hallucinating mentation. In *Sleep Research*, ed. M. Chase et al. Brain Information Service/Brain Research Institute.

Foulkes, D., and Vogel, G. 1965. Mental activity at sleep onset. *Journal of Abnormal Psychology* 4: 231–243.

Frankfurt, H. 1988. *The Importance of What We Care About*. Cambridge University Press.

Freud, S. 1959. Moral responsibility for the content of dreams. *Collected Papers*, volume 5. Basic Books.

Freud, S. 1962. *Civilization and Its Discontents*. Norton.

Frith, C. D. 1979. Consciousness, information processing, and schizophrenia. *British Journal of Psychology* 1324: 225–235.

Frith, C. D. 1987. The positive and negative symptoms of schizophrenia. *Psychological Medicine* 17: 631–648.

Frith, C. D. 1992. *The Cognitive Neuropsychology of Schizophrenia*. New Jersey: Lawrence Erlbaum Associates.

Frith, C. D., and Done, D. J. 1988. Towards a neuropsychology of schizophrenia. *British Journal of Psychiatry* 153: 437–443.

Fulford, K. W. M. 1989. *Moral Theory and Medical Practice*. Cambridge University Press.

Garralda, M. E. 1984. Psychotic children with hallucinations. *British Journal of Psychiatry* 145: 74–77.

Geertz, C. 1983. *Local Knowledge*. Basic Books.

Gillett, G. 1986. Multiple personality and the concept of a person. *New Ideas in Psychology* 4: 173–184.

Gillett, G. 1991. Multiple personality and irrationality. *Philosophical Psychology* 4: 103–118.

Gould, L. N. 1949. Auditory hallucinations and subvocal speech: objective study in the case of schizophrenia. *Journal of Nervous and Mental Disease* 109: 418–427.

Graham, G. 1998. *Philosophy of Mind: An Introduction*, 2nd edition. Blackwell.

Graham, G. 1999a. Self-consciousness, psychopathology, and realism about self. *Anthropology and Philosophy* 3.

Graham, G. 1999b. Fuzzy fault lines: Selves in multiple personality disorder. *Philosophical Explorations* 3: 159–174.

Graham, G., and Horgan, T. 1994. Southern fundamentalism and the end of philosophy. *Philosophical Issues* 5: 219–247.

Graham, G., and Stephens, G. L. 1994. An introduction to philosophical psychopathology: its nature, scope, and emergence. In *Philosophical Psychopathology*, ed. G. Graham and G. Stephens. MIT Press.

Green, M. F., and Kinsbourne, M. 1989. Auditory hallucinations and schizophrenia: Does humming help? *Biological Psychiatry* 25: 633–635.

Green, P., and Preston, M. 1981. Reinforcement of vocal correlates of auditory hallucinations by auditory feedback: a case study. *British Journal of Psychiatry* 139: 204–208.

Hacking, I. 1995. *Rewriting the Soul: Multiple Personality and the Sciences of Memory*. Princeton University Press.

Hamilton, J. 1985. Auditory hallucinations in non-verbal quadriplegics. *Psychiatry* 48: 382–85.

Heil, J. 1998. *Philosophy of Mind: A Contemporary Introduction*. Routledge.

Hemsley, D. R. 1982. Failure to establish appropriate response sets: an explanation for a range of schizophrenic phenomena. *Behavioral and Brain Sciences* 5: 599.

Hoffman, R. 1986. Verbal hallucinations and language production processes in schizophrenia. *Behavioral and Brain Sciences* 9: 503–517.

Hoffman, R., Oates, E., Hafner, R., Hustig, H., and McGlashen, T. 1994. Semantic organization of hallucinated "voices" in schizophrenia. *American Journal of Psychiatry* 151: 1229–1230.

Huizanga, John. 1959. Bernard Shaw's Saint. In *Men and Ideas*. Meridian.

Hume, D. 1739–40. *A Treatise of Human Nature*. Oxford University Press, 1978.

Jackson, F. 1982. Epiphenomenal qualia. *Philosophical Quarterly* 32: 127–136.

Jackson, F. 1998. *From Metaphysics to Ethics*. Clarendon.

James, W. 1918. *The Principles of Psychology*, volume 1. Dover.

Jaynes, J. 1976. *The Origin of Consciousness and the Breakdown of the Bicameral Mind*. Houghton Mifflin.

Junginger, J. 1986. Distinctiveness, unintendedness, location, and non-self attribution of verbal hallucinations. *Behavioral and Brain Sciences* 9: 527–528.

Junginger, J., and Frame, C. 1985. Self-report of frequency and phenomenology of verbal hallucinations. *Journal of Nervous and Mental Disease* 173: 149–155.

Kane, R. 1996. *The Significance of Free Will*. Oxford University Press.

Kinsbourne, M. 1990. Voiced images, imagined voices. *Biological Psychiatry* 27: 811–812.

Levine, L. D. 1988. *Bird: The Making of an American Sports Legend.* McGraw-Hill.

Linn, E. 1977. Verbal auditory hallucinations: Mind, self, and society. *Journal of Nervous and Mental Disease* 104: 8–17.

Locke, J. 1689. *An Essay Concerning Human Understanding.* Dover, 1959.

Ludwig, A. M. 1997. *How Do We Know Who We Are? A Biography of the Self.* Oxford University Press.

Lycan, W. 1981. Form, function, and feel. *Journal of Philosophy* 78: 24–50.

Maher, B. A. 1974. Delusional thinking and perceptual disorder. *Journal of Individual Psychology* 30: 98–113.

Mlaker, J., Jenstele, J., and Frith, C. D. 1994. Central monitoring deficiency and schizophrenic symptoms. *Psychological Medicine* 24: 557–564.

Margo, A., Hemsley, D. R., and Slade, P.D. 1981. The effects of varying auditory input on schizophrenic hallucinations. *British Journal of Psychiatry* 139: 122–127.

Maudsley, H. 1886. *Natural Causes and Supernatural Seemings.* Kegan Paul.

McGuire, P. K., Silbersweig, D. A., Wright, I., Murray, R. M., Frackowiak, R. S., and Frith, C. D. 1996. The neural correlates of inner speech and auditory verbal imagery in schizophrenia: Relationship to auditory verbal hallucinations. *British Journal of Psychiatry* 109: 148–159.

McKenna, P. 1994. *Schizophrenia and Related Syndromes.* Oxford University Press.

Miller, L. J. 1996. Qualitative changes in hallucinations. *American Journal of Psychiatry* 153: 265–267.

Mellor, C. H. 1970. First rank symptoms of schizophrenia. *British Journal of Psychiatry* 117: 15–23.

Mintz, S., and Alpert, M. 1972. Imagery vividness, reality-testing, and schizophrenic hallucinations. *Journal of Abnormal Psychology* 19: 310–316.

Modell, A. H. 1960. An approach to the nature of auditory hallucinations in schizophrenia. *Archives of General Psychiatry* 3: 259–266.

Mott, R. H., Small, J. F., and Anderson, J. M. 1965. Comparative study of hallucinations. *British Journal of Psychiatry* 12: 595–601.

Noonan, P. 1990. *What I Saw at the Revolution: A Political Life in the Reagan Era*. Random House.

Peirce, C. S. 1934. *Collected Papers*, volume 5, ed. C. Hartshorne and P. Weiss. Harvard University Press.

Penelhum, T. 1979. Human nature and external desires. *The Monist* 62: 304–319.

Penfield, W., and Perot, P. 1963. The brain's record of auditory and visual experience. *Brain* 86: 595–696

Plato. 1961. Theatetus. In *The Collected Dialogues of Plato*. ed. E. Hamilton and H. Cairns. Pantheon.

Plato. *Five Dialogues*. Hackett, 1981.

Posey, T. B., and Losch, M. E. 1983. Auditory hallucinations of hearing voices in 375 normal subjects. *Imagination, Cognition, and Personality* 2: 99–113.

Radden, J. 1996. *Divided Minds and Successive Selves: Ethical Issues in Disorders of Identity and Personality*. MIT Press.

Rapaport, J. 1989. *The Boy Who Couldn't Stop Washing: The Experience and Treatment of Obsessive-Compulsive Disorder*. Penguin.

Reese, W. D. 1971. The hallucinations of widowhood. *British Medical Journal* 210: 37–41.

Rund, B. R. 1986. Verbal hallucinations and information processing. *Behavioral and Brain Sciences* 9: 531–532.

Russell, B. 1981. *The Problems of Philosophy*. Oxford University Press.

Ryle, G. 1969. *The Concept of Mind*. Barnes & Noble.

Sacks, O. 1984. *A Leg To Stand On*. Harper and Row.

Sacks, O. 1989. *Seeing Voices: A Journey Into the World of the Deaf*. University of California.

Sartorius, N., Jablensky, A., and Shapiro, R. 1977. Two year follow up of patients included in WHO international pilot study of schizophrenia. *Psychological Medicine* 7: 529–541.

Sass, L. 1992. *Madness and Modernism: Insanity in the Light of Modern Art, Literature, and Thought*. Basic Books.

Schneider, K. 1959. *Clinical Psychopathology*, fifth edition. Grune and Sratton.

Sedman, G. 1966a. A comparative study of pseudohallucination, imagery, and true hallucinations. *British Journal of Psychiatry* 112: 9–17.

Sedman, G. 1966b. Inner voices: Phenomenological and clinical aspects. *British Journal of Psychiatry* 112: 485–490.

Shatz, D. 1986. Free will and the structure of motivation. In *Midwest Studies in Philosophy: Philosophy of Mind*, volume X, ed. P. French et al. University of Minnesota Press.

Shoemaker, S. 1986. Introspection and the self. In *Midwest Studies in Philosophy: Philosophy of Mind*, volume X, ed. P. French et al. University of Minnesota Press.

Sims, A. 1995. *Symptoms in the Mind: An Introduction to Descriptive Phenomenology*, second edition. Saunders.

Slade, P. D. 1976. Toward a theory of auditory hallucinations: An outline of a hypothetical four-factor model. *British Journal of Social and Clinical Psychology* 15: 415–423.

Slade, P. D., and Bentall, R. P. 1988. *Sensory Deception: A Scientific Analysis of Hallucinations*. Johns Hopkins University Press.

Snyder, S. 1974. *Madness and the Brain*. McGraw-Hill.

Spanos, N. 1996. *Multiple Identities and False Memories: A Sociocognitive Perspective*. American Psychological Association.

Stephens, G. L., and Graham, G. 1994. Self-consciousness, mental agency, and the clinical psychopathology of thought-insertion. *Philosophy, Psychiatry, and Psychology* 1: 1–10.

Szasz, T. 1996. *The Meaning of Mind: Language, Morality, and Neuroscience*. Praeger.

Taylor, M. A., and Heiser, J. F. 1971. Phenomenology: an alernative approach to the diagnosis of mental disorder. *Contemporary Psychology* 12: 480–486.

Wakefield, J., and Dreyfus, H. 1993. Intentionality and phenomenology of action. In *John Searle and His Critics*, ed. E. LePore and R. Van Gulick. Blackwell.

Wilkes, K. 1988. *Real People*. Clarendon.

Wing, J. K. 1978. *Reasoning about Madness*. Oxford University Press.

Wittgenstein, L. 1982. *Last Writings on the Philosophy of Psychology*. ed. G. von Wright and H. Nyman. University of Chicago Press.

Wright, D. 1969. *Deafness*. Stein and Day.

Zemach, E. 1986. Unconscious mind or conscious minds. In *Midwest Studies in Philosophy: Philosophy of Mind*, volume X, ed. P. French et al. University of Minnesota Press.

Index